260
W49r

122856

THE

C

THE RADICAL NATURE OF CHRISTIANITY

A Theological Study of the Supernatural Mission of the Christian and the Church

Waldo J. Werning

Acknowledgments

The author offers deepest appreciation to the eminent Christian workers and leaders who gave him their views on their mission or a special statement for use in this book. These the author views as unique and radical according to the terms employed in this book. Special gratitude is offered to the following men:

The Rev. Dr. Robert D. Preus, president, Concordia Seminary, Springfield, IL (Foreword)

The Rev. Dr. Harley Swiggum, founder and director of the Bethel Series, Madison, WI (Chapter 7)

The Rev. Dr. William Bright, founder and president of Campus Crusade for Christ, San Bernardino, CA (Chapter 10)

The Rev. Dr. Theodore Raedeke and the Rev. John DeVries, World Home Bible League, South Holland, IL (Chapter 10)

The Rev. Dr. Stanley Mooneyham, World Vision, Monrovia, CA (Chapter X)

The Rev. Robert E. Larson, Jr., executive director, CONTACT Teleministries USA, Inc., Harrisburg, PA (Chapter 10)

The Rev. Dr. William E. Welmers, professor of linguistics and African languages, UCLA (Chapter 11)

The Rev. Dr. Donald McGavran, Church Growth Institute, Pasadena, CA (Chapter 11)

The Rev. Dr. Jack McAlister, founder and president of World Literature Crusade, Studio City, CA (Chapter 11)

The Rev. Dr. Eugene R. Bertermann, executive director, Far East Broadcasting Co., Whittier, CA (Chapter 11)

The Rev. Dr. Eugene W. Bunkowske, consultant, United Bible Societies, Ibadan, Nigeria (Chapter 11 and 12)

The Rev. Dr. Francis A. Schaeffer, L'Abri, Huemoz nur Ollon, Switzerland (Chapter 12)

Three papers from the International Congress on World Evangelization in Lausanne have been used. They are "The Nature of Biblical Unity" by Henri Blocker (Chapter 8), "Contemporary Practices of Evangelism" by George W. Peters (Chapter 10), and "Methods and Strategy of the Evangelism of the Early Church" by Michael Green (Chapter 10). These lectures are now available in the book *Let the Earth Hear His Voice*, ed. J. D. Douglas, copyright © 1974, World Wide Publications, used by permission.

Table of Contents

Foreword

If one were hastily to survey the table of contents of Dr. Werning's new book or read it superficially, he might conclude that this is not a book on stewardship or missions. The reason for this would lie in the fact that stewardship in the church is in so many minds linked merely with economics, management, and business; and missions are so often linked merely with activism and administration. Dr. Werning, one of the foremost authorities on stewardship and missions, knows better than that. He knows well that missions and stewardship have their basis in theology, and the goals of missions and stewardship are always theological. If this is not the thesis of Dr. Werning's provocative and helpful book, it is a basic premise which permeates it. And this is its great value — its theological orientation. It speaks not only to the problems and challenges of our day, but answers many of the theological aberrations which tend to undermine the mission of the church.

This is not a handbook on how to do certain things, not offering us gimmicks, procedures, models, and the like, although there is much of practical material to be found throughout. It is rather a theology of church growth and missions. In this it is a refreshing change from so much of the literature on the subject. For the church lives by its theology. There is an old adage, *quod non est practicum non est theologicum*, "What is not practical is not theological." Or better óne might say, "All theology is practical." Dr. Werning not only believes this, but demonstrates it in the present book. By offering a theology of missions and church growth, he offers the most practical possible discussion of the subject.

Dr. Werning is eminently qualified to write such a book, which will be as helpful to laymen as to clergy. He has had years of experience as member and chairman of the Board for Missions of The Lutheran Church — Missouri Synod and of Lutheran Bible Translators. For over two decades he has served as a stewardship counselor in his church body — in two regions and at the national headquarters. His *The Stewardship Call* is a basic resource book for churches. Evangelical Christians are deeply in Dr. Werning's debt for this labor of love.

Robert D. Preus
Springfield, Illinois

Introduction

From the religious point of view, our century, now hastening through its final quarter, is in the main, a repetition of its predecessor. We observe a widespread radical change in attitude to life in general, a rejection of accepted moral values, a rash of theological novelties that turn out to be nothing more than regurgitations of ancient speculations. That is to say, we are experiencing an invasion of kinds of philosophy, commonly classified as idealism, realism, and pragmatism.

Bombarded as we are, some condemn at once as something evil all things that appear to be changes from what they have held to be true. Others flee into the past, hoping to find security there, thereby refusing to face the kaleidoscopic present. Most, it appears, turn skeptical and say with Pilate of old, "What is truth?" or they ask "What is 'God's power'? Where is 'God's goodness'?"

It is high time, therefore, to reexamine our beliefs and principles. We must be aware of the fact that God allows crises of authority so that we may realize the impossibility of living by natural powers and without moral absolutes. When skeptics openly question divinely inspired facts, the truth is often more readily proclaimed and discovered.

The God of history offers a Word that makes us painfully aware of the weaknesses of purely natural proposals for life. Divine truth is radical in contrast to other world religions and the antisupernatural contemporary theology and religious philosophy with their naturalistic emphases. Authentic Christianity, which involves the regenerating power of the Holy Spirit, the experience of conversion, the complete commitment of the evangelical Christian, and the spiritual basis for dedicated social service, is often not adequately presented as a live option.

Only authentic Christianity reveals Jesus Christ as Lord of all, who controls the destiny of nations, of powers, whether they be religious, cultural, political, or social. He is sovereign.

Who are the ones who will help their fellow creatures find hope in the midst of despair and find freedom from the shackles and prison of their own making? How will the churches develop Scriptural plans and implement God's divine strategy? How can we expect total mobilization of church members, and an emphasis on priorities that bring balance and joy to life? Only the Christian faith stands as a radical choice among all of life's options. Only Christianity helps to solve the basic conflicts of life. But are the churches equal to the urgent task when they are characterized by much inconsistency, indecision, deadening traditionalism, doctrinal divisions, inefficiency, and even unfaithfulness to God's will and Word? There is an urgency to answer these questions and to assess the present and future possibilities of churches to be the church—to disciple the nations. We ask, How radical is Christianity and the church?

This book promotes confrontation, not abandonment of responsibility. It declares the unchanging Word of God, not theological fads, and develops strategies based on divine will and revelation.

Salvation and the revelation of Christian truth are supernatural realities. Eyes and minds are limited to natural phenomena which can be seen and understood, but the Holy Spirit causes eyes to see and minds to comprehend those things that are not seen—the invisible forces which are divine and all-powerful. The church has been given the task to proclaim and live this truth—the entire Scriptures.

Christianity faces an hour of great opportunity for

shaping the destiny of the present age and of years to come, but there must be a determined will and great ability to do the job. Having passed the point for spending time on secondary issues, we ask for divine perspective, for spiritual insight, for commitment by Christians to be instruments of the life-giving Spirit of God in the fast-moving spirit of our age. True Christianity will offer a richness of life, a hope that warms cold hearts, and an unequaled, supernatural spiritual force that guarantees a future that surpasses the prospect offered by any other option.

What may we expect from Christian pastors and congregations? What is the duty of the churches, their institutions, their seminaries, and schools? This book is addressed to all interested Christians — laymen, lay women, youth, pastors, teachers, professors, church leaders — to propose a life commitment and to show the presuppositions by which Christian work might be undertaken to influence the world as God intended. The world needs people and churches which have supernatural power, a radical nature that includes divine intervention.

The word *radical* (from the Latin *radix*, meaning *root*) is used to refer to words such as roots, origins, and fundamentals. It denotes anything that proceeds from the root — relating to or springing from the essentials and basics. We are speaking here about something thoroughgoing but not "fanatical," which would be intemperate, violent, and unwise zeal and action. The root of human life is the Creator God, as to its source, strength, and purpose. Without connection with this˘ divine source — a radical essence — man is left with only natural powers.

Suggesting a theological basis for the self-examination and rethinking process necessary for Christian and church renewal, this book presents a practical strategy for continuing change and reform in individual lives and church structures. It makes a case for the radical nature of Christianity. These pages show the tie between pure doctrine and aggressive mission. Radical aspects are considered in theology, the local parish, the worldwide church, management of our resources, and the mission task. In a day of continued frustration over the lack of progress in many areas of church life, we seek to assess the situation honestly and make some daring proposals.

While the world offers nonradical or naturalistic answers to life's problems and piggy-backs on laws and powers which God has built into the world, the Christian reminds the world of the supernatural and radical powers and principles of the God who created, redeemed, and sanctifies men by His grace through faith in Jesus Christ, the only Savior of mankind. That's what this book is all about.

Chapter 1

A Radical Problem—Sin

Reviewing the 20 years after World War II, Walter Lippmann said: "We have tried so hard, we meant so well, and we have failed so terribly." A successful doctor, having achieved everything he ever dreamed, said: "All my success seems like an overripe apple rotting in my hands." Somerset Maugham said that if there were a TV set in his mind, he would be found guilty as a murderer, rapist, thief, and more.

Individuals throughout the United States and the world experience fear, dishonesty, falsehood, laziness, cowardice, treachery, cruelty, strife, dissension, lawlessness, and covetousness, while they hope for faith, love, truth, integrity, diligence, courage, thankfulness, kindness, restraint, and generosity.

Nations experience moral decline, immorality, violence, crime, racial hatred, student unrest and violence, disrespect for authority, cruelty, murder, wars, revolts, revolutions, unstable and unfaithful government, strikes, epidemics, business bankruptcies, raging inflation, unemployment, pornography, ethical breakdown in the arts and literature, divorce, infidelity, disruption of home and family life, shoplifting, thievery among employees, lies, communist infiltration, abuse of drugs and chemical acids, alcoholism, lack of patriotism, disobedience of children—*an explosion of evil.*

Signs of moral breakdown in Western civilization in our day are reminiscent of the five major causes for the decline and fall of the Roman Empire, summarized from the historian Edward Gibbon:

"1. The breakdown of the family and the rapid increase of divorce. 2. The spiraling rise of taxes and extravagant spending. Rome collapsed under the crushing twin burdens of creeping inflation and confiscatory taxation. 3. The mounting craving for pleasure, and brutalization of sports. 'Roman bath,' physical culture, and games were a primary concern. 4. The mounting production of armaments to fight ever-increasing threats of enemy attacks. 5. The decay of religion into myriad and confusing forms, leaving the people without a uniform religious commitment." These are all part of our own world—our society.

All this can all be lumped together as the *sin problem*. It is not the product of generations of indifference or failure of man to do his best, but of sin and human depravity— clearly manifested by weakened bodies, impaired minds, and disturbed emotions. This human sinfulness drives man to chase after three natural desires—to enjoy things, to get things, and to do things for self-indulgence.

This radical sin problem is predictable, for the Creator has provided the insights in His Word. This tells how man has always been inextricably enslaved by his own failure to save himself. People are willing to concede that the Bible's description of sinful man is accurate. In Genesis 8:21 the explanation of man's depravity is spelled out in these words: "The imagination of man's heart is evil from his youth." David, the great king of Israel, confessed: "I was shapen in iniquity, and in sin did my mother conceive me" (Ps. 51:5). Jeremiah, the ancient prophet, proclaimed: "The heart is deceitful above all things, and desperately wicked; who can know it?" (Jer. 17:9). Paul, the great missionary writer of many New Testament books, wrote: "Now the works of the flesh are manifest, which are these: adultery, fornication, uncleanness . . . idolatry, witchcraft . . . murders, drunkenness, revellings, and such like" (Gal. 5:19-21).

About 2800 years ago, at a time of great affluence in Israel, Isaiah ministered to the nation. He tells us in his book that the people had rebelled against God. They had

16

become thoroughly corrupt, a sinful nation, a people filled with iniquity. They had become guilty in three areas:

1. Political injustice. They sought bribes, had no concern for the helpless widow and orphan. They took advantage of the poor. Rulers were carousing. They made mockery of the law.

2. Moral corruption. Instead of justice there was murder. The land was plagued by property confiscators. Drunkards, defiant revelers, moral perverts abounded.

3. Spiritual poverty. They had taken on idolatrous customs. They placed wrong emphasis on the material.[1]

Origin of Sin

Man was created in the image of God, but this beautiful gift was damaged by his sin. The consequence of Adam's sin was that he was driven from the Garden of Eden, the place Adam and Eve had polluted by their disobedience.

Man has sought in many ways to restore Paradise, but all such efforts end in failure, for man's sinful nature will not enable him to have a paradise here.[2]

Sin subjected nature to a curse. Paul confirms this curse in Rom. 8:19-22: insects, weeds, earthquakes, hurricanes, and violent forces. Now death dominates human history. Man became a child of Satan. Sin robbed man of his original innocence and righteousness. Thus man's ability is fatally damaged and he is subject to frailties and impotence. Man's moral inability keeps him from hearing God's voice, believing, receiving, obeying, pleasing, knowing, confessing, and inheriting life eternal.[3]

Several things happened when Adam sinned: First, he died spiritually, destroying the relationship between himself and God; second, he became guilty and faced God's punishment, having broken the laws of God; third, he became self-centered, choosing his own determined way instead of God's way, so that self-centeredness became ingrained in man's very nature; fourth, he became enslaved to the devil, who had sought his fall and eternal destruction.

The tragic result of the Fall was threefold: *God-ward*, resulting in alienation from God; *self-ward*, resulting in condemnation and corruption, with the inner nature defiled; *Satan-ward*, resulting in enslavement to a subtle, cruel, crafty foe with endless temptations.

Man enslaved by sin is unable to better himself and society, for corruption rules his heart and brings him deeper and deeper into the mire of sin. In the Book of Romans, God gives us insight into the problem as He points out how man fights against divine truth. We learn how man turns away from the Light to the darkness of his own nature, as man changes God's glory into shame, and God declares man unclean. Man corrupted himself by his own lusts. Man refused to accept God's Word as true knowledge.[4]

Man, left to himself, repudiates the true God and goes into the "God business" for himself. He decides to live his own life, chooses what he wants, and makes up his own mind about what is right and wrong. These actions are a rejection of God as the Center of man's life. When the big "I" runs himself, man is driven to seek devious devices, such as drink, women, sleeping pills to lull him to sleep, pep pills to wake him up, and overdoses of stimulants and drugs to keep him going. He needs something to deaden his conscience or to fill his ego-needs. Man's sinfulness deadens and deceives by covering up his real intentions, by dressing himself in respectable clothes, by seeking popularity, and by telling outright lies. Man's sinfulness has a way of growing and increasing. His sins expand from the lesser to the greater.

The Wages of Sin

Sin pays wages—high wages! (Rom. 6:23a) It destroys character, reputation, and robs people of everything worthwhile in life. It robs people of their homes, their families, their companions, their means of livelihood, meaningful relations — their all. Its guilt is the most coercive emotion the human spirit has to bear, as it sinks man into depression. Guilt haunts a man, is a malicious accuser, shames him, and dulls determination and initiative. Sin in its aspect of unbelief and pride is the hostile "NO!" to God. Sin is man's rejecting of God, His love, mercy, and grace.

Sin is not merely a mistake or an unfortunate act or habit, but it is a deep-seated inward corruption. Sin not only estranges, but it also enslaves. It not only alienates us from God, but it also makes us captive to evil forces. It is an evil infection from which bad actions and habits spring.

The Great Evil Power

Behind the scenes Satan is working subtly through deceit and lies in order to capture the minds and hearts of people to fill the vacuum in their souls with misleading religious beliefs, leaving out God, who sent His Son to the cross for cleansing man of sin. There is a personal devil, just as there is a personal Savior. Satan is more than a doctrine, for he is a living reality — a danger. He is alive, and all people need to know what to do about him. Satan is a deceiver, a tempter, an adversary, a beast, the prince of the power of the air, and the god (evil force) of this world.[5]

The devil possesses radical power in the spirit world and is ready to exercise control over any person who will permit him. We should have a healthy respect for this enemy, know how he operates, be equipped and have a defense system for resisting him and protecting ourselves. The devil introduces his own ideas and tries to destroy the power of the Word of God.

Satan raged against Jesus, and he wars against us. He is our dedicated enemy. He disguises himself in other people, in circumstances, and in cunning suggestions.[6]

C. S. Lovett, in his *Dealing with the Devil*, states that "Satan uses every natural desire to enslave. It is natural to want to get ahead in this world, to stick up for your rights, to take advantage of opportunities, to protect yourself, to want the best, to put yourself first, to clutch what is yours, to want a good time, to cater to appetites and passions, to place self and family ahead of others, etc. . . . You see it is self-ambition that makes a man plunder; like scheming for another man's job. It is self-interest that makes him exploit someone else; a girl perhaps. It is self-satisfaction that makes him gossip; blind to the hurt it produces. It is self-praising that makes him occupy with the things of this world. Satan knows how to get us all to live for ourselves by triggering the NATURAL desires." [7]

Satan's work in the lives of people is extremely subtle and terribly powerful as he deceives the understanding. He makes things nearby appear to be great and great things to appear small. He hardens the conscience as he drugs the moral sense by encouraging self-indulgence and temporary pleasure — a kind of hypnotism. Here we see the supernatural power with which the devil and his evil spirits are invested, and the radical influence they have on our lives.

Paul warns that as the serpent subtly beguiled Eve, so our minds might be corrupted from the simplicity that is in Christ. Satan will injure youth, men, women, whole families. When we imagine we have risen to the highest point, we have in fact come terribly close to collapse and destruction.[8]

Needed: A Radical Recovery from Sin

The fall of man made it necessary to provide God's well-planned and perfect recovery program to give a release from the prison of sin. The radical plan includes calling sinners to repentance and faith in Christ, the Conqueror of Satan. Jesus steadfastly resisted the attractive overtures of Satan and by the power of the Holy Spirit enables us, too, to be victorious over him. God's Word, however, repeatedly warns us to be constantly on our guard against Satan's assaults.[9]

Paul did not recommend a social revolution in order to eradicate evil. He dealt with the spiritual roots of social evil — the selfishness and sinfulness of man. Where there is no firmness of faith in Christ, there is no order, but disorder. This disorder extends to the body, mind, spirit, and relationships — the entire social order. Man's sickness cannot be cured unless the total person is cured. The Bible's description of our depravity is part of a larger message of salvation. Men are lost, having missed God's mark because of their sins, but Christ has come to seek them out to be their Savior and Friend. Man by nature is selfish, ingrown, and carnal. But Christ has come to demonstrate a positive new wholeness via the drawing of the all-powerful Holy Spirit.

Today there is too great an emphasis in the churches on encouraging people "to be human," instead of reminding them to exercise the divine power within them. Every time we are reminded "to be human," we cry out that we are already altogether too human and that we need to be rescued from this human self-slavery. We need a special call to be partakers of the divine, through Christ, who dwells in the Christian by faith.

Those who emphasize the acceptance of existing human frailties without insistence on repentance and change, thus perverting the justice of God, should be asked whom they want in the driver's seat of their plane which they fly to Chicago, Dallas, Los Angeles, or New York: one who uses all human and spiritual resources to perform with great effort and integrity or one who hopes you will forgive his mistakes? Whom do you want to be your druggist: one who is completely committed to abiding by principles and standards which protect your health or one who knows that when he makes a mistake you will consider it simply human and forgive him? Society cannot and does not accept a careless pilot or druggist. Both need to repent and correct their weaknesses through the forgiveness wrought by Christ.

Because of the innate nature of human beings, they do not find it easy to repent of all the evil in their lives. If a person is not confronted with the real reason that he is uptight and has unresolved problems, there will be complete frustration and guilt. When he is confronted with the causes for his gnawing feelings of guilt and shame, he may become hostile, angry, suspicious, and defensive. But as he seeks the forgiveness of God at that point, he is led to find that the blood of Jesus Christ will cleanse him and release him from the wicked control of sin. He is enlightened by the Holy Spirit to see that God alone can and does rescue him from the destruction that awaits him.

Only those will be rescued who see their hopeless predicament and turn to God in confession and repentance. Unless a sinner sees God in His true qualities, he cannot see the true dimensions of his own need. If man will not understand the meaning of judgment on his sins, he will never come to an understanding of the meaning of God's grace to him.

One of the things desperately needed is a fresh understanding and sense of sin. This can never be obtained apart from a fresh appreciation of the price God paid to redeem man. Far too many possess an unbelievable smugness in regard to their condition as sinners. Some make a major sin of petty man-made rules and moral trivia, and in contrast engage in real sins such as greed, gossip, slander, immorality, prejudice, which they consider allowable because many others are doing them. They need to face the wrath of God to identify their behavior as contempt for His will and commandments. They will also learn that He is a God of forgiveness, proclaimed by Him in His reconciling Word, the life-giving Word. More, God offers him the power of the Holy Spirit to overcome the problem of sin. And as man asks, he will receive.

Notes to Chapter 1

[1] Is. 1:21-23; 2:6-8; 3:14-15; 5:8, 11, 12, 20, 22; 10:1-2.

[2] Gen. 2:10-14; Rom. 5:14; Tim. 2:13-14.

[3] Gen. 2:17; 3:17-19; John 3:36; 12:39; 14:17; Rom. 3:10-18; 5:12; 6:23; 8:7-8; 1 Cor. 2:14; 12:3; 15:50; Eph. 2:1-3; 4:17-19.

[4] Rom. 1:18-28.

[5] 2 Cor. 4:4; 11:3; Eph. 2:2; 1 Thess. 3:5; 1 Peter 5:8; Rev. 19:19.

[6] Matt. 13:19; Acts 5:3.

[7] C. S. Lovett, *Dealing with the Devil* (Baldwin Park, CA: Personal Christianity), p. 83.

[8] 2 Cor. 11:3.

[9] Luke 8:12; 22:31; 1 Cor. 10:5 ff.; 1 Peter 5:8-10.

Chapter 2

A Radical Solution to Man's Sin and Rebellion: God Enters the World to Give Man a New Life

In one way or another all people seek to understand the questions: Who am I? What is my reason for living? Who is my brother and how do I relate to him? How can I do my 'own thing'? How can I get the most out of life? How can I face death? What about a life hereafter? Is there a religion that can help me? What can Jesus Christ do for me? These questions focus on three crises of human life: Indentity, community, and power.

Man-made answers are not a solution to these demanding questions. Only a supernatural force will do. Why is Christianity the supernatural faith that is sufficiently radical to provide the kind of newness, creativity, direction, and power that is not just another religious view or philosophy of life but, in fact, The Answer?

The fundamental problem is not a rational one at all. The secret lies in a root change, a fundamental change in the human attitude toward God. Central in effecting the change is the incarnation of Jesus Christ — an unbelievable and absolute entrance of God into this world and our humanity in the Person of Jesus Christ. God sent His Son freely, sovereignly, graciously to unite Himself with human nature, entering the human race as Jesus of Nazareth. That's a stupendous claim, and that's radical!

Jesus Christ — The Center of History

God became a man in the Person of Jesus Christ to restore the broken fellowship with man. Christ lived a perfect life, and died as a substitute for us by paying the death penalty for our rebellion. He arose and lives to give us a new life of fellowship with God, now and forever, and with each other. The accumulated data of His claims and His character, together with the experiences of His followers and believers, lead step by step to the certainty that He was and is God. God's plan to keep the penalty from falling on man, as He sent Jesus to pay the full penalty of every sin of every man, allows man through faith to be converted and made new.[1]

Jesus declared Himself as divine and claimed the authority to forgive sins, recognized Himself as the Author of eternal life and the Judge of all men. Christ's attitude toward sin is a clue to His deity, as is His compassion for the needy and sinners. He came to earth to lay down His life for others that they might be restored and brought back to life. His death is evidence of God's love for sinners.[2]

Jesus' sharing our humanity and His taking on Himself our sinfulness resulted in His identifying with God as God our Father. To accomplish this, Jesus Christ, the Son of the Living God, became for some measurable time the rejected One, the Person who bore the wrath of God against the sin of the whole human race. It was He who on the cross cried out, "My God, My God, why hast Thou forsaken Me?" (Matt. 27:46) The Lamb of God became the slaughtered sacrifice as a payment for human sin. Jesus suffered the anguish of hell itself—a place where men are no longer children of God, but children of the devil, where God's wrath comes to take the place of His grace. We learn of the reality of hell from Jesus' suffering and cry. Nonetheless, the reality of hell is one of the greatest problems to any man's faith. Those outside the Christian faith who scoff at this reality and reject it express a very natural reaction. Although it is a frightening, even repulsive fact to many, we see the shape of hell as we stand at Calvary, as the Bible so forthrightly declares that it is a fact.

The force of Christ's cross lies in the destruction of all

of sin's power. The majesty of the cross is seen in the divine offering, and the beauty of the cross in its finality, for here we perceive a sacrifice that was "once for all." The power of the cross lies in the resurrection of Jesus Christ. Fortunately, the image and power of the cross penetrated our world of unreality and fantasy, which refuses to acknowledge the presence of sin. The cross is God's evidence that we are worth everything to Him. The same cross which makes us feel the reality of sin also makes us feel the reality of our significance to God.

No force has been able to overcome the absolute power of Christ's cross. Its influence is greater than the influence of any philosophy, university, or government. Before He was ever nailed to it, Jesus foretold the power and the love of His cross for the good of men: "And I, if I be lifted up from the earth, will draw all men unto Me" (John 12:32). A Christianity robbed of the cross is a pseudo-Christianity, a Christianity robbed of its radical nature and power; and a world robbed of true Christianity is a world with absolute hopelessness. What the sun is to the solar system, what the needle is to the compass, what the heart is to the body—that the cross is to a man who would find any hope or positive direction in life.

God's great recovery program shows us how He has met every one of the needs of mankind, including regeneration, deliverance from the power of the enemy, and growth and maturity in living for God. This occurred as Christ suffered *for* us—our Substitute (regenerating us); as Christ suffered *as* us—our Representative (dealing with our old man and carnality, making possible our freedom from the power of sin); and as Christ Crucified comes *in* us—our Indweller (dealing with the new man, who is "Christ in us").

Since man of himself does not and cannot possess righteousness, Christ imputed His righteousness to him. As he becomes enlightened by the Holy Spirit, he joyfully accepts this righteousness which justifies him. It is free. This is not just restoration or reformation, but the creation of a new person with a new nature, new life, new relationships, new direction, new insights, new citizenship, new power. It is not the turning over of a new leaf. It is a new man (2 Cor. 5:17-19; Eph. 2:8-10)

Man must be rid of his own garments, his own proclaimed goodness, his own works, by which he wants to appease God. Naked in his sin and weakness, he is given Christ's spotless garment of righteousness through faith. An artist wanted to paint a picture of the Prodigal Son and found a man on the Bowery. This man went to his room, shaved and put on his one suit, and met the appointment. When the artist saw him, he said, "I can't use you!" So we must come to Christ as we are, not in our best personal dress and personal good, but lay claim to nothing except Jesus' merit and righteousness.

Many people are very uncomfortable before such exclusive claims of Christianity, but have they really checked their pulse or felt their mortal body recently; have they taken stock of their lives, words, and actions?

Christianity—The Radical Solution

What is it that makes Christianity so radical among all other religions? Christianity cannot be tested for truth, for it is the test of lesser truths. No light can be thrown on it, for its own Light blinds the investigators. As Christ is accepted by faith, Christianity tells more about the universe, about history, and about man's condition and meaning than all the other facts accumulated in human history.

Christianity ends all religious speculation and demolishes all man-made religious ceremonies and sacrifices. It shows that the presence of God is not remote and distant, but that the very life of God is evident in the world. Man-made religion supposes that the true God is yet to be discovered. Christianity shows that He is here. Man is not the ultimate master of his own fate. More is required than man's innate knowledge of the Law and to love mercy and to be just. Christianity stands above and beyond moralization and human comprehension.

Christianity provides a faith with an understanding of history that is authentic, for the Gospel alone interprets man's longing and effectively describes God's method of fulfillment for man.

Christianity is not simply another way of looking at life or a system of philosophy. It is not a way of living or a code of ethics. Many people are friendly towards Christianity because they see in it a philosophy of ethics they like, but they are not convinced of its truthfulness and doubt that it is intellectually respectable. They stumble at the insistence that Jesus is the one and only Savior and Lord. The absoluteness of the Christian faith is a stumbling block to man as he naturally feels and thinks.

Christ does not merely add something to the sum total of the world's knowledge or religion, but is the Center of all truth and life. When Jesus is the Center of our lives, the life focus changes from the sensuous to the spiritual. Christianity is not a call to adjust the spiritual to the secular, but a call to conform the secular to the spiritual.

Instead of accepting the various sentimental and philosophical evaluations many make of Jesus, we look at the real Jesus—the One the Bible describes so completely. The reason why many do not accept Christianity is to be found, not in Christianity but in their own philosophy of life. The fault does not lie with the Light but with those who prefer to make their decisions in their self-created darkness.

Sincerity, often urged as a valid criterion, is not sufficient. Some sincere students surmise that God grades on a law-oriented curve. Hence they conclude that somehow they will make it. But God tells us in the Scriptures that He grades on the basis of absolute sinlessness.

Some others have the tragic, mistaken idea that we must choose between what we choose to do and inevitably be happy in enjoying the supposed good things in life or, on the other hand, choose to do what God wants us to do and so be miserable because the intellect is not challenged while joy is lost. To this view Christianity responds: The intellect and joy are sharpened and heightened through conversion and faith in Christ.

Christianity provides a Savior who gives to all a love that cannot be measured, a wealth that is beyond all earthly treasure, a purity that knows no defilement, a righteousness that cannot be blemished, a strength that never diminishes, a resource that is never spent, a joy that never ends, a hope that never fades, and a faith that overcomes all.

How radical is Christianity? The path of restoring man from brokenness to healing begins and continues in conversion and regeneration. This means a liberation from the evil forces which enslave, and a healing that originates in a victory which Christ won for man. Man's guilt brings emotional destruction such as fear, anxiety, worry, resentment, hatred, an inferiority complex, and self-centeredness. The essence of spiritual sickness is the estrangement of a person from God. The essence of Christianity is freedom from the power of sin.

Free from Sin to Serve God

It is faith that embraces forgiveness. It assures that the chains of sin are loosed. Jesus said, "If the Son, therefore, shall make you free, you shall be free indeed" (John 8:36). This is a freedom which only Christ can give—a freedom which leaves "no condemnation . . . for the law of the Spirit of life in Christ Jesus has made us free from the law of sin and death" (Rom. 8:1-2).

The nature of this freedom involves both a "from" and a "to." Through faith in Christ the believer is:

1. Free *from* sin's guilt and condemnation, free *from* the power of Satan, and free *from* the fear of death.[3]

2. Free *to* obey God's Word, free *to* live in the will of God, free *to* love our fellowman, and free *to* serve God in witnessing, service, and firstfruit giving.[4]

Freedom means commitment to God and His will. People with a commitment to the Christian faith are free to work creatively in a world which is enslaved to Satan and evil forces. There is no religious bondage more demoralizing than that which occurs when someone forgets God's Word and constructs his own religion and supposed freedom. God offers no one license to do his "own thing" or do what is "right in his own eyes," precipitating for him one crisis after another. Ours is a unique freedom which leads to responsible action in the Christian ministry and mission.

Faith Is the Hand That Accepts What God Gives

Christianity is a faith, and the Christian life is a witness of that faith.

It is solely from its object—Jesus Christ—that faith derives its value.

Faith is the hand that grasps the faithful promises of God. It takes the gift of being justified from sin, of being sanctified and enabled to live the Christian life. Faith is based on an objective Word of God—the Gospel message. Christian faith is the only proper attitude toward life.[5]

Faith is the "Yes!" of the heart. Faith takes from God the strength to walk the servant path. "He has by His own action given us everything that is necessary for living the truly good life, in allowing us to know the One who has called us to Him, through His own glorious goodness. It is through Him that God's greatest and most precious promises have become available to us men, making it possible for you to escape the inevitable disintegration that lust produces in the world and to share God's essential nature" (2 Peter 1:3-4 Phillips).

Christianity is faith in the Triune God, the Father, the Son, and the Holy Spirit. Religion without Christ leaves man with faith in himself. Christianity is man's commitment of mind and heart to the one true God. It is not a philosophy, or psychology, or a human welfare program, but rather a supernatural, divinely created entity.

"Believe!" is the constant reminder. If you believe God's promises, you have the secret of life. So Jude writes: "Build yourselves up on the foundation of your most holy faith and by praying to the Holy Spirit to keep yourselves within the love of God" (Jude 20-21). Moreover, faith can never overdraw its account: "He who supplies seed to the sower and bread for food will supply and multiply your resources and increase the harvest of your righteousness" (2 Cor. 9:10 RSV).

Proverbs 3:5-6 suggests three steps of faith to gain the promise that God shall direct the Christian's path: "Trust in the Lord with all your heart; and lean not unto your own understanding. In all your ways acknowledge Him, and He shall direct your paths." Step 1: Trust in the Lord! Believe in God with all your heart. Step 2: Don't depend on your own understanding or insight. Step 3: In all your doings and accomplishments, acknowledge God. When success comes, you will not claim the big reason to be your intelligence, education, cleverness, good fortune, or innate ability. Rather, faith will acknowledge God's grace and goodness. Thus God will direct man's path.

Faith is active in prayer: "What things soever you desire, when you pray, believe that you will receive them, and you shall have them" (Mark 11:24). "If you can believe, all things are possible to him that believes" (Mark 9:23).

Christian faith is triumphant: "Above all, taking the shield of faith, wherewith you shall be able to quench all the fiery darts of the wicked" (Eph. 6:16).

There can be no true discipleship without profound and unquestioned faith in Christ, our Savior. He who lives in us by faith is stronger than the world (1 John 4:4). Faith opens doors where despair has closed them. Only he who believes in God's miraculous power is a realist.

The centrality and power of faith given to man by God's grace is evident in Ephesians 2:1-10. Before God works His miracle of conversion and regeneration, man is a spiritual corpse — dead in sin, obeying Satan, his life expressing the evil within by doing every wicked thing to which passions and evil thoughts might lead. But God, who is rich in mercy, loved us so much that even though we were spiritually dead He made us alive by His grace, expressed by the demonstration of the Holy Spirit, and lifted us up from our spiritual grave to be alive in Jesus to serve His purposes. By grace we are saved through faith, not of ourselves, for it is a gift of God, not of works, lest any man should want to take credit for what he is doing. We are God's "workmanship," created in Christ Jesus unto good works — for producing and expressing Christ's life within us in our actions. We do not do good works in order to *be* saved, but because we *are* saved. An apple tree does not become a live apple tree by producing apples, but because it is alive. The Christian alive in Christ does good works because he has the power and life of Christ by faith within him.

Summary of Christianity

Summarizing man's potential for good in this life, we review the vital truths that man needs to learn about himself:

1. God created man in his own image for fellowship with Him.

2. Man fell into sin and became estranged from God, with no power left to him to save himself, and for His

rebuilding is entirely dependent on God's grace and mercy.

3. God responded by paying the highest possible price, the sacrifice of the life of His Son for redeeming man.

4. Anyone on earth can be brought to a saving relation and vital union with God by the means of grace, through faith in Jesus Christ.

5. Redeemed people are members of the body of Christ, the invisible church, and are to be brought together in congregations — visible groups — for edification, fellowship, and Christian service.

6. Believers by the power of the Holy Spirit are to witness to the Savior and share the saving Gospel of Christ locally and to the ends of the world.

Notes to Chapter 2

   [1] John 10:10; Acts 2:23; Col. 1:19-20a; Rom. 5:8; 1 Cor. 15:3-4; 1 Peter 2:22.

   [2] Mark 2:5; 10:45; John 5:27; 10:15, 28.

   [3] Rom. 6:14; 8:2; Col. 1:13; Heb. 2:14-15.

   [4] Rom. 6:16, 18, 22; 7:6; Gal. 5:13; Eph. 5:15; James 1:22-25; 2:12; 1 Peter 2:16.

   [5] John 5:24; Acts 26:18; Rom. 1:17, 11-20; 4:3, 22-25; 5:1; Heb. 11:8.

Chapter 3

Regeneration Leads to a Radical Life: The New Man in Christ Overcomes the Old Man of Sin

Man without Christ is hopelessly in bondage — enslaved to the devil, the world, and his own sinful flesh. Man with Christ is a free man but is engaged in an endless *civil war* between his new self and his old self. His old self is overcome but still dangerously active to negate the free and new man.

The Bible tells how the new man of the Christian overcomes the old man. St. Paul writes: "I have been crucified with Christ; it is no longer I who live, but Christ who lives in me, and the life I now live in the flesh I live by faith in the Son of God, who loved me and gave Himself for me" (Gal. 2:20). When a person is crucified, he should be dead, but Paul stated that he lives after crucifixion (with Christ). However, Paul said that it was not really he that was living, but that Christ lived in him. Therefore the life that he lived thereafter in his body was no longer controlled by sin or evil forces, but lived in the faith of Jesus Christ, now Lord of his life. The old self died as a controlling force when the new self was born.

In order to understand man's dilemma, to know man's real enemy, and to understand the tense, never-ending struggle, let us look at both the old man and the new man as to their intrinsic natures.

The Old Man

Natural man, the old man or old Adam, as the Scriptures call him, is an unreformable rebel, who is thoroughly corrupt, driven by his deceitful lusts. The natural man's mind is at war with God and resents God. He is ignorant of the things of God and lacks appreciation of God's authority and goodness. "The natural man receives not the things of the Spirit of God, for they are foolishness unto him; neither can he know them, because they are spiritually discerned." Because of his carnality, natural man is dangerous and deadly, for he is bitterly antagonistic and destructive of true spirituality. This carnality is a love of and desire for what offends God, and it turns away from God and toward sin.[1]

Natural man stands before God empty-headed and empty-handed. He has neither word or deed which can be accepted by God, and has "fallen short of the glory of God" (Rom. 3:23).

Know the nature of our old Adam: He is conceited, arrogant, haughty, and a willing lackey for the fraudulent maneuvers of the devil, who suggests that he be lord of the world. He wants to be more than a creature, more than the Omnipotent's servant, as he shuns humility. Intoxicated with greed and self-sufficiency, he is a slave to the devil, the sinful world, and his own self. He refuses God's foundation and thus loses the floor under his feet. Self-glory and deception hide behind his whitewash and pious words. With his proud thoughts he can neither know God's feelings about him, nor try to establish a proper relationship with God or his fellowmen. His will is perverted, his judgment perverse, and his impulse evil. The old man, with his unrestrained desires, craves privileges, rejoices in exalted positions, selfishly complains about his lot in life, and uses his time and abilities for his own interests. He doubts the wisdom of God, or anything that would lead to a new life.

The manifestations and evil results of the natural man are named in Gal. 5:19-21: impure thoughts, lustful pleasure, idolatry, hatred, fighting, jealousy, anger, complaining, false doctrine, drunkenness, envy, and wild parties. The natural man seeks to cause carnality in a Christian in whose life the power of Christ is becoming weak, with the result that the Christian experiences little desire for the study of God's Word, leads a poor prayer life, and succumbs to worry and fruitlessness in witnessing.

The natural man doesn't know what he is missing: He is like a man born blind who doesn't miss color or a man born deaf who doesn't miss beautiful music. Consequently, the old man tries to crowd Christ out of our hearts, our heads, our habits, our homes, and even out of our theology.

By nature our human wills are certainly in bondage to our bodies and glands, to say nothing of the major forces in the world. Our emotions sink like a stone in water in the midst of great earthly turbulence. Men's minds, not led by the saving love of God, wander in the jungle of confusion and reject God's clear revelation of Himself. The need for a radical dynamic in life is not met by natural, intellectual, or social elements, for all fail to deal with the basic weaknesses and corruption of humanity.

The New Man

When a man is in Christ, he is a new creature, for old things have passed away. He has put on the "new man which is created in righteousness and true holiness." Becoming a new man—a son of God—is a supernatural gift. "Unless a man is born of water and of the spirit, he cannot enter into the kingdom of God" (John 3:5). Through faith and baptism we become a new being destined not to serve sin but to serve God. Jesus calls this being born again! [2]

The new man is born of God. Just as a carpenter cannot build a tree, so we cannot by any human efforts become children of God, but must experience the new birth. God lets the Word, the Gospel, the Eternal Seed, fall into the heart of man and fasten on the heart as the Holy Spirit is present and makes a new man.

The new man in Christ has the following attributes:

— He is spiritually minded and subsequently disposed toward the things of God.

— He has spiritual understanding and is able to discern and to discriminate between what is of God and what is not.

— He manifests the fruits of the Spirit even in times of severe testing, stress, and strain.

— He yields himself as a channel for good by the Holy Spirit.

— He offers up spiritual sacrifices unto God.

— He lifts the fallen, restores those overtaken in sin, and exhibits the spirit of meekness.

— He is dead to the things of the world.

— He is alive to Christ, to "the things which are above." [3]

As new men, our eyes become the eyes of the resurrected Christ to exhibit His sympathy and tenderness, our lips to speak His messages, our ears to be sensitive to every cry of spiritual need, our minds to plan His work, our hands to act at the Savior's impulse, our feet to keep in step with Christ throughout life.

The new man is one who is unwilling to be deterred from the path of God to what is materially profitable or morally degrading. He holds convictions that are neither for sale nor open to compromise. He shows himself to be a willing servant to all men but a slave to none.

Being the new man means that we have turned the management of our lives over to Jesus Christ. Christ Himself is formed in the Christian by faith and will be magnified in his body and life.

The new man in us is the very life of Christ. Led by the Holy Spirit, we can know and experience God's plan for our lives. We can do all things through Christ, who strengthens us. This, too, is what is radical about Christianity.[4]

Civil War Between the Old Man-New Man: Sinner-Saint

The nature of the Christian's tension is that he is both sinner (old man) and saint (new man). This does not mean that he is partly a sinner and partly a saint, but altogether in his natural self a sinner and altogether in Christ a saint. Luther's classic phrase is that the Christian believer is "saint and sinner at the same time."

The Christian who does not understand the old man-new man tension or civil war will be hopelessly frustrated in his wavering between hot and cold service to Christ, and his high and low spiritual moods.

The old man is the origin of man's evil desires. He is never eradicated but remains in the believer during his whole lifetime. The believer's new nature, the new man, was given to him by faith in Christ. This nature is incapable of sin and leads the believer to think, say, and do those things that are pleasing to God. These two natures in each reborn person are diametrically opposed to each other. The result is a radical conflict.[5]

That the believer has been justified, made right in his relation to God, does not mean that he has outgrown the need for forgiveness but rather that he knows to whom to go for it.

Since the Christian's righteousness is Christ's righteousness, in which the Christian is clothed by faith, it is always entirely an imputed righteousness. Our old nature is never completely eradicated, even though it is mortified daily. Jesus, who hit history with such an impact that He split it into two periods, gave man his new nature—the new man, a child of God and heir of heaven.

Romans 6—8 offers important insights into the two natures of the believer, telling how the victorious life in Christ can be lived. Sin's power was broken when we were baptized to become a part of Jesus Christ, through whose death the power of our sinful nature was broken. Our old desires and sinful habits are to be nailed to the cross of Jesus. Our own sin-loving nature died as dominant, as Christ ended sin's power over us. Sin should no longer control our body or our organs. We should be unresponsive to sin and its allurements.

We should be alive to God, tools in the hands of God to be used only for good purposes. We should now be enthusiastic servants of our new Master, Christ, and all that is right and holy. God has freed us from slavery to our old nature. He has destroyed sin's control over us. The Holy Spirit places us under the control of our new nature—the new man. By God's grace we are now His children by adoption. This status we reflect in our new life-style.

The believer is always both flesh and spirit, sinful and righteous, dead and alive. Because of his struggle with the old man, the Christian never obtains, but is always pressing toward, the goal of the high calling in Christ Jesus (Phil. 3:14). He is ever striving toward "mature manhood, to the measure of the stature of the fulness of Christ" (Eph. 4:13 RSV), so that his "manner of life" may "be worthy of the Gospel of Christ" (Phil. 1:27 RSV).

Notes to Chapter 3

  [1] Rom. 7:14 ff.; 8:7; 1 Cor. 2:14; Eph. 4:22.
  [2] 2 Cor. 5:17; Gal. 3:26-28.
  [3] Rom. 8:6; 1 Cor. 2:15; 12:1, 7, 31; 13:4-7; Gal. 5:22-24; 6:1; Col. 1:9;
3:1-4; 1 Peter 2:5.
  [4] John 14:20; Eph. 1; Phil. 4:13.
  [5] Rom. 8:9; Gal. 5:17; Eph. 4:22-25; 2 Peter 1:3.

Chapter 4

A God of Justice and Love:
The Message of Law and Gospel

God, whose attributes include justice and love, has provided the killing power of the Law and reviving power of the Gospel to produce healthy Christians. Unfortunately, the failure to understand or to distinguish between Law and Gospel creates spiritual patterns that are humanistic, fearful, confused, or legalistic.

There is nothing so sick about a Christian life or a congregation's existence that a proper distinction between and use of the Law and the Gospel cannot cure. The Spirit of Christ witnesses to the power of His death and resurrection in us by wounding and healing, by making poor and making rich, by defeats and victories, prepared for us for a joyful and fruitful Christian life.

Many Christian lives are shapeless or weak because they have not experienced the exposure of the Law or the healing power of the Gospel, or because there was a failure to use the Law to prepare the way for the blessings of the Gospel. To use the Law only to admonish man to do loving acts is like telling a soldier whose legs have been shot off to get up and march. To use the Gospel only to send man on God's mission when he does not recognize his death-rattle is like trying to communicate with a person in a deep slumber.

The reconciler and sanctifier is always God Himself, and He has given His Word of Law and Gospel to make men spiritually awake and strong. The basic business of the church is to provide the richest supply of the Word for every member to gain maximum growth and knowledge, faith and godly living. It is God's plan and will that is to be proclaimed to people.

Law

The Law is God's sharp and straight edge to show us how crooked and ragged we are, not a motivation for getting people to act as Christians. Law frustrates, angers, rebuffs, and never gives an inch. God works His miracle of grace by using the Bible to correct man's blindness and show him his true condition. God's holy law is particularly important in driving this fact into man's consciousness.

Man tries to be satisfied with himself because he measures up to man-made standards of decency. Humanistic standards are brought down to that which is humanly achievable, because man has determined that God can't expect more than is possible for him. The Law is a corrective for such false views of life.

The Law looks good when needed to get a job done, but inside it tears one apart. In a way, it just stands there, nagging. It provides no power or willingness to do what it demands. The Law condemns the transgressor to the dungeon of his deserved doom, but having sealed his fate, it knows of no way to let him escape from its justice. In the very act of demanding love, "it works wrath" (Rom. 4:15). It can never create the joy and strength that constitute the very life and essence of expression of the Christian life.

The Law supplies a knowledge of sin, demands perfect obedience, and pronounces condemnation on all who do wrong. It tells man of his failure. When the law of God curses one's life and he sees that God desires perfect love and will be satisfied with nothing less than that, the blindfold will be ripped off and he will see himself as a sinner before the holy God. Presenting the Law makes man hostile, defensive, desperate, hurt, wounded, and gives him no place of escape to which to run.[1]

Furthermore, the Law is the righteous, unchanging will

of God that reveals what is to be the quality of man in his thoughts, words, and works in order to please God. It threatens transgressors with God's wrath, and with earthly and eternal punishment.

The Law, then, serves as a curb to crucify man's evil flesh, as a mirror to reveal his sins, and as a rule to regulate and direct his life.[2]

There are three extremes to be avoided:

(1) Forms of antinomianism, i. e., a confusion of the Law and Gospel or teaching and using the Gospel without the preparation provided by the Law. The fact that we are not under Law as a means for justification does not, therefore, imply that we are not under the Law as a guideline for leading a godly life. Erasing the guideline would displace lawfulness with lawlessness, and obedience by apostasy. Holy love can withhold nothing due to God or man. The avoidance of Law or considering Law to be relative and incidental or setting aside all absolute Law leads to justifying one's continuing in sin in one way or another. Both Law and Gospel are to be used side by side in proper order and with correct distinction. God's grace and forgiveness is to be proclaimed also on the basis of Law, sin, and accountability to God, followed by the Gospel of forgiveness.

(2) Legalism is the misuse of the Law, trying to use the Law to produce change in the new life. It is vital to see clearly that the Gospel alone will produce faith, love, patience, joy, and humility, which are marks of the Christian believer. The Law is easily used as a club when there is a lack of Christian behavior. The user of the club has forgotten that Christian behavior is the fruit of Christian faith. Legalism is a continual threat to believers, causes dissension, robs believers of joy, and is corrected only by God's grace through the Gospel by the ministrations of the Holy Spirit.

(3) Moralism, using the Gospel to teach morals, such as

honesty, courage, and love. Thus each Gospel story becomes a moral to teach and each good Biblical character becomes only a moral model to be copied. This process slowly drains the flesh and blood from the Holy Scriptures until they emerge as models in a morality story. Proclaimers must avoid comfortable little homilies, stylistically prefaced by Bible texts and emotionally framed to insulate the hearer against the judgment and grace of God. This will lead to the establishment of new codes as laws of the church. Respectability and love for others will become the aim of Christian living. Thus, believers will ultimately be tempted to trust in their supposed goodness.

Gospel

The Gospel is the Good News that Christ has paid the full price for the guilt of man's sins, has obtained the righteousness and forgiveness of sins that avails before God, and has won for man eternal life. The Gospel is so complete that it asks from no one meritorious good works in order to gain salvation. No work can do what the Savior has already done freely. The Gospel constrains and produces good works, but does not demand them from anyone to become justified before God.

Why not? Divine love revealed in the Gospel caused the Man of Sorrows to be wounded, bruised, suffer, and die in man's stead. Man wants to provide a deposit to his credit and thereby try to satisfy some of the demands of God. But the Gospel informs us that God already has on deposit the riches of His grace for man's spiritual poverty.

For reason the Gospel is simply impossible to believe: So much is given, so much endured, so much offered that only the Holy Spirit can move anyone to accept the Gospel. It is an offense to the contemporary Sadducee. The Holy Spirit puts an end to raving, accusing, and explaining, rationalizing, and pencil-sharpening. The Gospel gives, forgives, and gives again. The love revealed in the Gospel is not simply an attitude which Jesus taught, but it indicates the essence of His very being. Love is the fountain of God, and it pours out all of His gifts into the hearts of believers through the Holy Spirit. Love is God's "drawing power" —not only drawing men away *from* sin, sinful pleasures and earthly temptations, but also drawing them *to* Himself and all that He wills.

Indeed, God's love is His rich endowment of gifts to believers; it produces security, peace, joy, power. His love is His energy imparted to our lives. This makes it possible to use these gifts faithfully.

The Gospel is relevant to the needs of man in this world, for it conveys the *only* solution for man's basic problems— reconciliation with God. It offers release from sin by the Atonement made by Jesus Christ. It alone offers comfort to the troubled, the worried, the hopeless, and those frightened by the prospect of death.

The world of unbelief encourages man to overlook or excuse human weaknesses, but the Gospel says, "God will forgive you through Christ." The world of unfaith encourages deception and dishonesty, but the Gospel says, "Repent and receive the forgiveness of sins."

The world of misbelief encourages rationalization in renaming sin only a mistake, but the Gospel says, "Christ has freed you from your sins by grace through faith."

Relation Between Law and Gospel

The Law is an x-ray on the heart. In contrast, the Gospel is light and warmth for the heart. The Law curbs sinful man outwardly; the Gospel frees him inwardly. The Law demands good works; the Gospel gives power to do good works. The Law shows man his sins; the Gospel teaches him how he may be cleansed from his sins.

Preaching of the Law *only* inevitably results in hypocrisy or in despair or cynicism; the preaching of the Gospel *only* results in indifference, apathy, and smugness. A healthy Christian is produced when Law and Gospel are used properly, according to their intended use. After showing us what is wrong with us the Bible does not leave us standing there alone, without hope. The very moment the Scriptures reveal to us our sickness, they present us with effective medicine for our cure.

The Law as a mirror may reveal a dirty face, but it cannot wash it. The Law serves to reveal to man his shortcomings, but it lacks the power to cleanse and make man whole. Only the Gospel absolves and cleanses. Two great principles are operative: the law of God and the grace of God.

The cross of the Lord Jesus is God's greatest demonstration both of His law and of His grace. The Law prepares the soil of the hearts for the Gospel seed of God's mercy in Jesus, while the Gospel is God's action, intervention, and work to renew, ennoble, and enable man as a child of God.

Reading the Bible a man said to his wife, "Mary, if this Book is right, we are wrong." He was reading the Law. Reading further, he said, "Mary, if this Book is right, we are lost." That's still Law. Reading again, he exclaimed, "Mary, if this Book is right, we are saved." He was then reading the Gospel.

Compare the Law and Gospel in the way they *affect* and *influence* man:

Law	Gospel
Destroys	Heals
Works on behavior	Works on the heart that directs behavior
Makes people sad, mad, bad	Makes people glad
Freezes the heart	Thaws the heart
Challenges *man*	Challenges *God*
Weight is on *man*	Weight is on *God*
Puts a man on his own (do something)	Puts a man in Christ (faith)
Multiplies sin	Erases sin

The temptation has always been to try to repair the Gospel with the Law when the Gospel seems to fail to give the desired helps. Human rules and proposals are created in support of the Gospel. Man has a built-in radar for Law, since a remnant of the Law reposes in every human heart. Compare the *results* of the Law and Gospel:

Law	Gospel
Sorrow	Joy
Bondage	Freedom
Death	Life
Cannot please God	Please God
Self-effort	Faith

The New Testament process for the good life is both practical and simple: the growth and development of God's people according to God's design based on the Gospel of forgiveness. God's Word tells us to renounce all merely human criteria that judge people according to psychological, sociological, religious presuppositions which may appear correct in themselves but which the miraculous Word of God makes totally irrelevant.

Security and Joy: A Life of Repentance and Forgiveness

God calls for radical surgery for people who wish to live a healthy and whole life — spiritual surgery. As we understand the indescribably heinous character of sin, we will not only abhor it but also seek to put it out of our lives. Spiritual surgery is *repentance*, which means, "changing one's mind . . . rethinking . . . turning around." The Biblical concept of repentance denotes a very radical change, a definite turn from every thought, word, deed, and habit which is known to be wrong.

Jesus was intolerant of sin: "Except you repent, you shall all likewise perish" (Luke 13:3). It is not a question of whether we like repentance or not, but of whether we want to find real joy or not.

The only method of dealing with sin is to confess it, for God is faithful to forgive our sins and to cleanse us from all unrighteousness (1 John 1:9). Regeneration and repentance is as necessary for eternal life as natural birth is to physical life.

How do we repent? First, there must be sorrow for sin, as tears flow, the heart is broken, and the spirit is low. The mind and will are involved in confessing sin, turning away from wicked ways, turning to God for pardon, cleansing, and restoration. Second, there must be a change of mind, a fundamental reorientation in our thinking, a 180-degree turnabout.

Godly repentance means to stop habitual sinning, to turn and go the other way—to change the way of life. Repentance is a change from a carnal attitude and hostility towards God and His will to worship, love, and obedience to God and reliance on Him.

Repentance also means to "put away the strange gods among you, and be clean, and change your garments," as Jacob ordered his household. Man is an idol-maker, no matter how civilized he is, even after Christ has entered his heart. Repentance should unmask all contemporary forms of idolatry.[3]

Repentance and confession mean opening our lives to God, making no excuses but fully recognizing our lost condition. It is not the sorrow of being "caught," but sorrow over the sin itself. Repentance is vital, for "if we say that we have no sin, we deceive ourselves, and the truth is not in us" (1 John 1:8).

We should vow to deal radically with sin: Confess our guilt to God, who alone can help us get rid of sin and guilt. Name every known sin, repudiate it, and trust God for deliverance from it so that as far as we know we do not continue in any sin consciously or deliberately.

If you are proud, call it pride. If you pity yourself, call it self-pity. If you are jealous, call it jealousy. If you are envious, call it so. If you are resentful, admit it. Don't rename your temper indignation, but call it temper. If you talk about other people to their hurt, call it gossip. Let us be candid and speak frankly to God about our personal sins, for the blood of Jesus cleanses from sin. Instead of covering up sin and trying to find a fancy name for it, call it by its name and get rid of it by the grace of God.

Repentance consists in man's renouncing all self-sanctification and self-help. Repentance leads to actual acknowledgement of sin and dealing with it in a definite manner. The repentance of a Christian is serious, yet at the same time joyful because it is rooted in forgiveness. The Lord's gracious call to repentance leads to the marvelous and freeing experience of forgiveness by the mercy of Christ. This gives a new direction to life.

The Power of Forgiveness

The Gospel of forgiveness is intimately related to an active Christian life. Forgiveness is the stepping-stone to responsibility. When our burden is lifted, we are prepared to lift the burden of others. As sin alienates from God, so forgiveness reconciles to God. Forgiveness through Jesus is the monumental difference in our capacity, by grace through faith, to be what God called us to be, to fulfill our eternal destiny.

The Christian's daily life is a call to salvation, to eternal life, to sanctification, to patience and suffering, to servanthood, to a glorious hope. Each new word or experience of forgiveness from God is a new assurance that He works out His fatherly purpose in our lives.

God's Word and His forgiveness produce powerful and effective action for good in the total life of the child of God. If we had not been forgiven and assured of full deliverance from all our guilt for Jesus' sake, it would be impossible for us to live as God's children. Without having forgiveness we would be so hopelessly burdened by our guilt that we would not care whether we pleased God or not, for we would still regard Him as our enemy. Since He has forgiven us, all this is changed, and we have every reason to love Him and gratefully serve Him by His grace.

Those whose life has not been touched by God's forgiveness are filled with uncertainty, fear, anguish, doubt, and rage. God's complete and constant forgiveness alone covers all our failures to live this life as a child of God. Through this forgiveness, as often as accepted, there results release from guilt, renewal of life, and fresh motivation to continue to serve God and our neighbor.

Christ's forgiveness moves us to live a forgiving life. Our forgiving grows out of God's action whereby He freely by grace forgives us through faith in Christ. The forgiving life reflects and illustrates God's forgiveness for man. By living the forgiven-forgiving life, we display what God has done for us. The forgiving life binds wounds and heals divisions among people. Forgiveness restores harmony and heals the hurt, and fellowship is restored.

Since the forgiving life cannot be perfect in this world, it needs daily forgiveness for vitality and faith. The forgiven-forgiving life is the true life, made in God and with God. Such a life strives to glorify God and serve the neighbor in all things.

The word of forgiveness is essentially the word which graciously lays hold on man's life to lead him out of captivity to liberation. A change of regime takes place. Once man belonged to sin and death; now he belongs to Him who is liberator and his new Lord. The power of sin and death is broken, and the power of Jesus is established.

The forgiving word is no empty word, but a word that possesses power and strength. Through it our Lord summons us to His work. Forgiveness gives an inevitable desire for a new life.

God's liberality in forgiveness is so great that we cannot fully comprehend it, for "as far as the east is from the west, so far has He removed our transgressions from us" (Ps. 103:10-12).

Notes to Chapter 4

[1] Rom. 3:20; 7:7-11; Gal. 3:10-12.
[2] Rom. 7:7, 13; 8:7; 1 Cor. 9:27; Gal. 5:19-25.
[3] Gen. 35:1-5; Joshua 24:14.

Chapter 5

The Word Above All Words: God Himself Speaks to Man

God—the Holy Trinity, the Father, the Son, and the Holy Spirit—made the world, sustains it, and directs the processes of nature by His Word. He brought life into being by His Word. The Word through which He builds and supports the world is Jesus Christ. God had the first Word, and He will have the last Word. His Word establishes the truth about everything.[1]

God's Word is the written Scriptures, of which the Holy Spirit is the Author. The Bible is God's Book of Letters written to us at the hands of His human instruments— apostles and prophets. His purpose in writing to us is to reveal His will and His plan for mankind, to warn against sin and rebellion, and to tell how in divine love He deals with sin and sinners. His Word is "able to make us wise unto salvation through faith which is in Christ Jesus" and is "profitable for doctrine, for reproof, for correction, for instruction in righteousness" (2 Tim. 3:15-16).

As man encounters the Word of God, the conditions are brought about to give him true fellowship with his Lord and Maker. The Word of God is the ground on which man meets his Lord in judgment and in mercy, for it gives man knowledge of his corrupt nature by the Law and provides forgiveness and a new life by the Gospel.

All things in life stand in relation to the Word of God, because Jesus Christ became flesh so that everything human, no matter how sinful and corrupt it may be, can be reached and grasped by the divine Word and made into God's own. There is no subject so remote that the power of His Word cannot reach and accept it.

The Word of God clearly reveals the existence of God the Father, the Holy Spirit, and the Son, Jesus Christ. "God, who at many times and in many ways spoke in time past by the fathers and by the prophets, has in these last days spoken unto us by His Son" (Heb. 1:1-2 RSV). Between the origin of man and the destiny of man stands the cross of Jesus Christ. He who spelled out the destiny of man through the crucifixion, death, and resurrection of His Son, Jesus Christ, has also given us the infallible record of the origin and history of man in relation to the Creator.

According to the Scriptures, God is revealed as the Father, Son, and Holy Spirit—three Persons but only one essence. Our forebears sought to formulate the Scriptural description of God (incomprehensible by human reason) in the Athanasian Creed, one of the three ecumenical creeds. It describes the essence and nature of the Triune God.

Man meets the God of the Bible as the God of love through His Son. The Holy Spirit will convince him of the fact that the written Scriptures are the infallible, written Word of God. The actual content of the divine Book is God's redemptive revelation, the Gospel of God's grace to be proclaimed to all men blinded by sin, that they may be made to see and believe that Jesus is indeed the Christ, the Son of the living God, and that believing they may have life eternal through faith in His name.

It is an incredible and radical book. No one would ever believe it or accept it if God its Author, the Holy Spirit and the Lord Jesus Christ, would not guide and direct his mind and heart, as He did the human writers of the Holy Scriptures.

"What no eye has seen, no ear heard, nor the heart of man conceived, what God has prepared for those who love Him, God has revealed to us through the Spirit. For the Spirit searches everything, even the depths of God. For what person knows a man's thoughts except the Spirit . . . which is in him? So also no one comprehends the thoughts of God except the Spirit of God. Now we have received not the spirit of the world, but the Spirit which is from God, that we might understand the gifts bestowed on us by God. And we impart this in words not taught by human wisdom but taught by the Spirit, interpreting spiritual truths to those who possess the Spirit" (1 Cor. 2:9-13 RSV).

The governing means for the church are not external power and coercion, not human commandments and wisdom and skill, but only the Word of God. God preserves and governs His church solely through His Word, not by the power of men.

Authority

Some people said about Jesus: "No man ever spoke like this Man. . . . He speaks with authority." Jesus was different because of His authority, as His voice — His Word — is the authoritative voice with corresponding power to perform.

When we read the Bible, we find the authority of God on every page. We find from Genesis to Revelation that the divine authority is expressed through the Godhead, the Father, Son, and Holy Spirit. Throughout His time on earth the Son, Jesus Christ, especially asserted His authority: "All authority is given unto Me. . . . I will raise up this body. . . . I will build My church." The Lord has committed all authority to His Son. He is the final authority. He is Lord.

The solution for the problems of individuals, nations, and the church is to acknowledge Christ's authority not only in their lives but also in His infallible Book, the written Scriptures.

The written Scripture is the supernatural message and Word upon which the Christian faith is built. It records

55

history which tells of God's supernatural power and acts in dealing with His people in precise points of their lives and in relationship to Him. This seems strange to a world that accepts very little of the potency of God's wisdom. How radical that power is, can be seen by Jesus' statement: *"All* power is given unto Me in heaven and on earth" (Matt. 28:18). Man imprisoned in his naturalistic and materialistic cell tries to lock the door to all radical and miraculous actions of God, but the miracles which began at the creation of the world and are revealed in His Word continue to bless His people today.

Attacks upon the authority and authenticity of the Scriptures as the infallible Word of God run counter to the Scriptures' own unbroken testimony to their complete integrity. It does no honor to Jesus Christ to minimize the written Word that He, the Incarnate Word, so constantly taught. Only grievous harm will come to Christians and to Christian communities when doubt is cast upon the unique authority and nature of the Scriptures.

No teaching of Jesus Christ on any subject is clearer than His teaching on the Bible complete authority. Heaven and earth would pass away before the dotting of an "i" or the crossing of a "t" would disappear from the Law. He rebuked His disciples for not believing all that the prophets had spoken. He argued that Scripture cannot be broken, dissolved, or discarded. Jesus' teaching about the authority and inspiration of the Bible must be freely admitted by all those who can comprehend words and ideas. To accept Christ's lordship and at the same time to reject the authority and inspiration of the Bible is being inconsistent. If the written Word is not correct testimony of what it claims for itself, then how can we be sure that it is correct in its testimony concerning Jesus? [2]

Apart from the written Word, we can know neither the Incarnate Word of history nor the Incarnate Word of a living faith created by the Holy Spirit. Apart from the

Bible, Christ no longer remains the Jesus of history, and apart from the Jesus of history we could never know the Christ of our faith who is living, moving, and working in the world today.

Our faith in Christ does not exist in a vacuum but looks at the Word, which depends on the general reliability of the New Testament documents as evidence from history: the historical evidence of Christ's sinless life, the genuineness of His miracles, His stupendous claims as to His own Person, and His bodily resurrection from the dead. Confidence in Christ grows as we involve ourselves with the Word.

As we read the Word, we are always driven back to the real issue: "What do you think of Christ? Is He our divine Lord, or is He not? Is He the final authority over our life and thought, or is He not?" The Son of God bears the hallmark of authority. We can't run away from accepting the authority of the Word because it will follow us wherever we go. That's why when the authority of the Word is under debate, polarization shifts quickly from issues to personalities, then to anarchy.

As Jesus went on record to stamp the writers of the Old Testament as reliable, we read: "Beginning at Moses and all the prophets, He expounded unto them in all the Scriptures the things concerning Himself." His exposition of the writings of Moses and the prophets were so authoritative that His followers said to each other: "Did not our hearts burn within us as He talked to us on the road and explained the Scriptures to us?" Later, as we read in the same chapter in Luke, He even certified Moses as His first writer: "This is what I meant when I said, while I was still with you, that everything written about Me in the law of Moses, in the prophets, and in the Psalms, has to be fulfilled." To those who would argue about the authority and authenticity of the Word, He said: "O fools, slow of heart to believe all that the prophets have spoken!" (Luke 24:25-48).

God-Inspired and Infallible

The apostle Paul, too, believed that he had a divine revelation of truth which he was obliged to preach and to write under the inspiration of the Holy Spirit. His claims to such authority and inspiration of the Scriptures he himself wrote are the same as those of other New Testament writers.

The Biblical writers not only assume but declare that the Bible is the literal, inspired Word of God and is completely accurate in all details. These men give credit to the Holy Spirit for having inspired such accuracy.

To be sure, the object of saving faith is the Lord Jesus, not the Bible. However, Christian faith finds this precious object in the Holy Scriptures, the ultimate and only reliable source which reveals Jesus to man in human language.

The word *inspiration* is taken primarily from 2 Timothy 3:16: "All Scripture is given by inspiration of God." The term *inspiration* denotes a "breathing" and the accurate recording of that which God wanted the author to write. Those who find the doctrine of inspiration incredible must also find the possibility of supernatural intervention in human affairs incredible. Peter wrote these enlightening words on this subject: "The prophecy came not in old time by the will of man, but holy men of God spoke as they were moved by the Holy Ghost" (2 Peter 1:21). The inspiration of the Bible reveals that it was written in the very words of God's choosing.

The church, while affirming clearly that the Scriptures are inspired and without error, has wisely refrained from attempting to define the precise manner in which God inspired the Scriptures. We know that verbal inspiration means that the very words of Scripture in the original documents were chosen by God. The claims for verbal inspiration obviously apply only to the original documents, not to the copies which are available today. However, it is

58

truly amazing that our present-day copies have been kept surprisingly free of apparently even minor mistakes.

The inspiration of the Bible does not set aside the human side, for the Scriptures have both divine and human aspects. The writers of the Scriptures were not mere pens or near-robots in the hand of God. Verbal inspiration is not even a cousin of the dictation theory, for the rich and extensive variations in style would naturally suggest that God employed the personalities of human instruments. The divine-human side of the Scriptures can be understood as being somewhat like the divine-human side of Christ. Although human, Christ was without sin, perfect. Although human instruments were used, the writings are also without error, perfect.

God's Word is not to be judged by human reason, but by the Word of the Creator Himself. It was written for the good of all men and is to be shared to the ends of the earth.[3]

Is this bibliolatry or worship of a book? Not at all, for we worship the Savior revealed in the Book. Jesus fully affirmed the verbal inspiration of the Scriptures, but He was not literalistic. He did not confuse the external legalistic observance of the Scriptures with the complete acceptance of the Scriptures. His denunciation of "following the letter of the Law" did not mean that the Law did not have a letter to be followed, but rather that the spirit and application did not stop at the letter. Yet He could talk about the importance of dotting the "i's" and crossing the "t's." Such problems disappear when one observes clearly what inspiration is and what it is not. The question is not whether we find difficulties in the Bible but whether we find God Himself telling us that these words and these books are inspired and without error—and whether the Scriptures themselves claim a comprehensive divine approval of the autographs. After all, only the divine Author is in a position to say whether these writings possess supernaturally guaranteed truths and facticity.

Inerrancy is intimately related to the inspiration of the Scriptures, but it is not the decisive aspect of inspiration. That aspect is authority and power: The inerrancy of the Scriptures is tied to faith and results from the authority and power of the inspired Scriptures. This implies that God is able to express His greatness and truthfulness in accurate human language.

The mere fact that we are unable to solve every linguistic difficulty and to answer every question now does not justify the inference that such problems are incapable of solution. As we see something seemingly wrong in the Scriptures, the cause could be that some copyist made a minor mistake or that we need new glasses — better spiritual insight. Any approach to the Scriptures or method of interpretation which makes the Scriptures something less than trustworthy does not take them on their own terms. We believe the Bible reveals God's truth because we believe in God, the Author of the Bible. If we believe in the integrity of the person, we also believe in the integrity of his writings. Thus we refuse to accept as truth a Christ stripped of His divine and human attributes, as well as the authenticity of His Book.

When present-day critics press their case against the inerrancy of the Bible, they don't cite new discoveries in science and archaeology, but they point to those passages that have been known to the church down through the centuries. In addition they depend on the theories of scholars who basically have ignored the testimony of the Scriptures themselves. Inerrancy "hang-ups" are not new.

Let it be said that inerrancy is not conceived as an insistence on a complete and verbatim matching of quotations in the New Testament taken from Old Testament statements. Moreover, inerrancy does not imply that all passages of the Scriptures have to be interpreted in a literal way, for inerrancy is not at odds with figurative language. Nor is inerrancy destroyed by a writer's use of certain expressions of his day or descriptions of nature that are not stated in "scientifically precise language." He who holds that there are errors in the Bible has arrogated to himself knowledge he does not actually possess. Small wonder that negative judgments against the Bible have had to be modified or revised over and over again.

We conclude that the inerrant Bible ("not liable to prove false or mistaken and therefore trustworthy in all its contents") is reliable in all the historical and scientific contents in its records, does not contradict itself. Its reliability extends equally to all the words of the original documents. It is not surprising that Jesus, the Author, told Satan that man should live by "every word that proceeds out of the mouth of God" (Matt. 4:4). A faithful Christian will exhibit similar confidence in the trustworthiness of all the contents of the Scriptures.[4]

Teachings and Doctrine

All teachings—doctrines—of the Scriptures must be accepted. Martin Luther said: "He who denies Christ in one article or word has in this one article denied the same Christ who would be denied in all articles; for there is but one Christ in all His words, collectively and individually."[5]

We dare not be selective, accepting some doctrines of the Scriptures and rejecting others, yet claiming to recognize them all as teachings of God's Word. God was most jealous of His doctrine, and He often spoke through His chosen prophets against false prophets, even threatening them with fearful punishment.

Jesus showed both a positive concern for His doctrine and a negative concern regarding all false doctrine. We learn from the Scriptures that there is such a reality as doctrine, pure doctrine, false and pernicious doctrine, and corrupt teaching. We learn that schisms exist in the church because of false doctrine, that Satan is behind false doctrine, that Christ teaches what is true and false doctrine, and that we need to pray for the gift and preservation of pure doctrine.[6]

False doctrine originates with the devil. It is sin. It is dangerous to the soul. It must be exposed, avoided, and rejected.[7]

Faithful Christians will be gracious yet unyielding when doctrine is concerned, for Christ has attached Himself to His propositions. Christ's doctrine is not to be altered or adjusted, but it is to be trusted. Possible attitudes toward doctrine and truth are the following: suppress the truth, obey the truth, walk according to the truth, resist the truth, err from the truth, know the truth, be made free by truth, be established in the truth, be of the truth, have truth in us, and do the truth or live according to the truth.[8]

The Teacher Is the Holy Spirit

Only the Holy Spirit can lead us into the truth and doctrine of God. Unaided, our minds cannot grasp spiritual truths. By ourselves we are easily satisfied with guessing and groping after the truth. The natural mind by itself can produce problems rather than solutions.

The Holy Spirit is not a substitute for careful thinking. Man is not absolved from the duty to think. But the Holy Spirit alone gives man spiritual understanding and wisdom.

The Holy Spirit illuminates, teaches, and guides the Christian by the Word. The Holy Spirit provides the Christian with insight and understanding. Without the Holy Spirit man understands the Scriptures only intellectually. The Spirit gives understanding spiritually. When the Word of God is studied and heard with open ears and hearts, the Holy Spirit will give repentance, followed by the putting away of idols, then by spiritual revival and the outpouring of God's blessings.[9]

The most revolutionary force in the world is the Word of God. It should be read to be wise, for it instructs the mind. It should be believed for man to be spiritually strong and safe, for it teaches the heart.

The Spirit's blessings which flow from searching the Scriptures are seen in Ps. 119 as cleansing, understanding, comfort, fellowship, liberty, peace, and guidance. It is the glorious authority and guide for life itself. Its promises, encouragements, exhortations, and gifts should be applied to one's life.

Special Power for Forgiveness

God offers His great blessings through the Gospel. God uses means through which He gives the blessings of forgiveness: His Word joined to Baptism and to the Lord's Supper. God offers, conveys, and assures His grace through His Word of promise, and He seals and applies these blessings.

A Washing of Regeneration

The Great Commission tells us to teach all nations, "Baptizing them in the name of the Father, and of the Son, and of the Holy Ghost." What God commands and institutes in His Word is precious to man. The Ethiopian and the jailer were instructed, and then they received the blessing of Baptism.[10]

Repentance, Baptism, and forgiveness of sins belong together: "Then Peter said unto them, repent and be baptized, every one of you, in the name of Jesus Christ for the forgiveness of sins, and you shall receive the gift of the Holy Ghost. For the promise is unto you and to your children" (Acts 2:38-39). The unique blessing of salvation is shown in John 3:5-6: "Except a man be born of water and of the Spirit, he cannot enter into the kingdom of God"; Acts 22:16: "Arise and be baptized, and wash away your sins, calling on the name of the Lord"; 1 Peter 3:21: "Baptism doth also now save us."

Our relationship in Christ is cemented through Baptism: "Know ye not that so many of us as were baptized into Jesus Christ were baptized into His death?" (Rom. 6:3); "For as many of you as have been baptized into Christ have put on Christ" (Gal. 3:27); "Christ also loved the church and gave Himself for it that He might sanctify and cleanse it with the washing of water by the Word" (Eph. 5:25-26). The Word of God, through faith which trusts God's Word of promise, gives us forgiveness, life, and salvation.

The Lord's Supper

Our Lord Jesus Christ instituted the Lord's Supper by taking the bread and wine, giving thanks, saying that we should eat and drink, for this is His body and blood given and shed for the forgiveness of sins. Paul told the Corinthians; "The cup of blessing which we bless, is it not the communion of the blood of Christ? The bread which we break, is it not the communion of the body of Christ?" (1 Cor. 10:16).

This radical eating and drinking must be approached with faith and self-examination, for "whosoever shall eat this bread and drink this cup of the Lord unworthily shall be guilty of the body and blood of the Lord. But let a man examine himself, and so let him eat of that bread and drink of that cup" (1 Cor. 11:27-28).

Thus the blessings are the forgiveness of sins, strengthening in our faith, and bearing testimony of a common faith and bond in Christ.

Notes to Chapter 5

1 Ps. 33:4-6; 147:15-19; John 1:1-5; Heb. 1:2-3.

2 Matt. 5:17-19; Luke 24:25; John 10:34-35.

3 Ps. 119:104; Matt. 5:14-16; 28:19-20; Luke 24:25-44; John 8:31-32; Acts 17:11; Rom. 15:4; 1 Cor. 2:13-14; Eph. 4:17-18.

4 Two notable books recommended on this subject are: J. A. O. Preus, *It Is Written* (St. Louis: Concordia, 1971); Norman Geisler, *The Theme of the Bible*, (Chicago: Moody, 1968).

5 Ewald Plass, *What Luther Says* (St. Louis: Concordia, 1959), p. 407, No. 1202.

6 Luke 4:22; Acts 17:19; 1 Tim. 1:10; 4:6; 6:1; 2 Tim. 4:3.

7 Jer. 23:31-32; Matt. 7:15; 13:25; 15:8-9; John 8:43-45; Rom. 16:17; Gal. 3:1; Eph. 4:14; 2 Tim. 2:16-18; 2 Peter 2:1.

8 Deut. 12:32; 1 Kings 8:56; John 8:32; Rom. 1:18; Gal. 5:7; James 5:19; 2 Peter 1:12; 1 John 1:6, 8; 2:21; 3:19; 3 John 4.

9 John 14:26; 16:13; 1 John 2:20, 27.

10 Acts 8:26-39; 16:25-33.

Chapter 6

God's People in a Natural-Supernatural Community—Congregations of Believers

The Gospel and the church are essentially related. The Gospel points to and maintains the church, and the church is derived from the Gospel. The Gospel gathers and edifies the church as the body of Christ. The church has the mission given by Christ Himself to proclaim the Gospel, the Good News.

God has established the church as the mutually functioning members of the body of Christ. All authority is derived from Christ, the Head, and is exercised in His name and by His Spirit. The church is a bride of whom Christ is the Bridegroom, a flock of which Christ is the Shepherd, a royal priesthood of which Christ is the High Priest.[1]

The church has been entrusted with the ministry of reconciliation, as believers are responsible to Christ and responsive to the world. Leaders are to equip saints for the ministry and mission under the Word, and every believer is to develop and use fully his gifts of the Spirit within the church.[2]

The church is not a man-made organization, but one with a divine origin, God alone being its Architect and Builder. To Him alone the church owes its existence, on Him alone it must depend for its continuance, and to Him alone it owes its loyalty, faithfulness, obedience, and commitment. The church, in the primary sense, consists of only those who believe in Christ, as the Holy Spirit calls, gathers, enlightens, sanctifies, and keeps them in the true faith through the Word.

God has entrusted to His church the proclamation of the Gospel, through which He builds and extends His kingdom. The true marks of the church, by which it is known and identified, are the means of grace—the Word of God, Baptism, and the Lord's Supper. He deals with men only through these means.

The church seems to be a paradox: It is divine, a body in which the Spirit of God Himself lives and acts; yet it is human, made up of men who are faulty. The church is spiritual, yet earthly. It is holy, yet it is composed of sinful men. It experiences the same kind of dichotomy as the Christian himself, who is both sinner and saint.

Because of the human involvement, the church cannot escape some form of embodiment or structure. It must take shape in this world, made up of people, programs, meetings, buildings, finances, and tasks. It is spiritual, yet expresses itself through earthly institutions. It is divine, but functions through human beings. Never, however, dare the organizations, the machinery, or the institution take the place of Christ or assume their own authority.

The church is both visible and invisible. The *invisible* church denotes all true believers in Jesus Christ; the *visible* church or congregation contains both believers and hypocrites, but this fact in no way destroys the authority and power of the church.

The strength of the church is found in its doctrine, its worship, its fellowship, and its witness. The church is a believing community, a worshiping community, a loving and edifying community, a serving community, and a witnessing and missionizing community. The church is an organism with the Gospel as its vital force.

The church is a theocracy, an institution under the rule of God, not a democracy, although it is an institution governed by people. The principal function of the people is to seek direction from God and to submit to His Word under the guidance of the Spirit.

The life of the church constitutes worship of the Triune God, study and proclamation of God's truth, use of the means of grace, the ministry of intercession, the joy of fellowship with other Christians, and outreach into the world with the Gospel.

Members of the Christian church are to sustain each other by using individual gifts for the good of all, as seen in Romans 12: Prophecy, speaking the Gospel to each other; service, ministering to special needs; teaching, training each other in the Word of God; exhorting, furnishing spiritual power by encouragement; liberal giving; guiding in the areas of worship and service; showing mercy, acts of caring and welfare to the underprivileged. Members of the church minister to each other in many ways (2 Cor. 8:1-5). Each member is responsible for the life of the other. Mutually, they are custodians and agents of God's great gift in Jesus Christ.

The church is the only institution on earth whose sole mission is to help men find God and eternal life through Jesus Christ.

Search for Renewal

The primary need for the congregation and its leaders is to decide whether they will accept God as the only authority. Required is a vigorous process which calls for specific diagnosis of the objectives, goals, and organizational structure.

It is not unlikely that some of our church life is actually contrary to our objectives and goals. We will do well to listen to the provocative criticisms of John Heuss: "We churchmen are working industriously away in our churches without asking too many critical questions about what we are doing and why we are doing it. . . . The Christian religion alone can save the world. The average American is not impressed with this claim at all. The reason is that he simply cannot imagine the local church in his community in any such heroic and revolutionary role. . . . The saving Gospel does not square with what he sees before his eyes. . . . If we can work with divine discontent and candid self-criticism, God will help us make His Gospel heard yet by a generation that suspects at present that we do not mean what we are saying." [3]

What are some of the basic church problems today? Unfortunately, too often churches in general have succeeded in pulling Christian men and women away from community and civic affairs, society, and the world to grasp them for the women's kitchen crew, the men's dartball or bowling team, the ushers' team, the finance committee, or endless church meetings. Possibly some of the programs to which people are harnessed are carried on because no one has the courage or initiative to replace them with something more productive. There are also those who hold entrenched positions or views which they do not want disturbed. Some spend endless time in programs organized to fight crises instead of planning to overcome basic diseases and problems.

When a congregation gets to the place where it no longer innovates but only imitates or perpetuates, nothing short of a vigorous renewal that grows out of a genuine repentance and rediscovery of its roots will lead to a radical renewal. Too easily the congregation may forget its Gospel mission and servanthood, revere its expendable forms, and crawl fearfully into the shell of self-preservation. At such times churches go through the forms of faith and worship thoughtlessly and take comfort in their religious routines with ideas rigidly locked in place. Meantime, spirits are sagging. Sometimes churches seem to be merely recepticles of traditions left by our fathers with all the freshness gone.

Members need to examine whether their congregation has become so inverted, so caught up in internal maintenance and procedure, so entrapped in preserving and proliferating a cumbersome self-serving organization and financing costly ecclesiastical apparatus, that it has practically lost its integrity and missionary purpose. Traditionalism and "programitis" can become so dominant that the church can be estranged from her Lord, and the sovereignty of the Lord replaced by the sovereignty of the programs and workers. When the church is separated from her mission, members are separated from members, and the proclamation of the Gospel is separated from its implications for the Christian's life in society.

Someone has called this an "activities orgy," which has resulted in pastors majoring in administration, while Christians are exhausted and neglect their spiritual life. What now confronts us is a materialistic society, almost devoid of Christian penetration, a Christianity equated with church attendance, a nonspiritualized church program carried through by hard work rather than by the Spirit, programs executed totally within the walls of the church building and yielding a loss of mobilization and sense of direction.

We could quarrel with the thesis that new programs are the greatest need of the church, for perhaps the greater and more basic need is the renewal of individual Christians. Our problem cannot be solved by perfecting the organizational machinery of the congregation, but by renewal through the Gospel.

Clergy and lay leaders alike need to discern the Biblical image of the congregation, realize that it collides with cultural images, allow the Word to dictate decisions, and stand firmly against the competing cultural images which blunt the authentic ministry of the Word. However, destruction of a specific form or program does not automatically settle the problem, for new forms and programs may become even a greater problem.

Another problem is the church building itself, which may stand in the way of radical renewal. Some expand church facilities at the expense of the congregation's vital witness. We cannot afford to allow anything, particularly buildings, to blind us to our primary Gospel objectives. Not only have church buildings imprisoned the finances of congregations, but they also have imprisoned the laity in the church operations by a wrong focus. Before plans are made for new structures, an exhaustive study needs to be made of the purpose and function of the building in relation to the primary tasks of the congregation.

The word *ecclesia* (church) never refers to a building in the New Testament. Nor is there any exhortation for Christians to erect a building for a place of worship. The emphasis was on people as seed. With the right kind of seed, there will be church growth. The local church was the people meeting in someone's house: the church in the house of Priscilla and Aquila, etc. First-century Christians met in temples, in rented halls, in private homes, out in the open, or wherever they could. Special buildings for congregational groups probably did not appear until several centuries later.

We do not jump to the conclusion, however, that buildings are useless or contrary to the purpose of the church. We are simply noting that vigorous churches existed and grew with great vitality without erecting a church building.

Effective Programs That Contain Biblical Concepts

The New Testament does not indicate any mandatory form of church polity or organization or program which is to be imposed on the church today. We note that the worship, witness, and welfare of the church is a primary consideration in the development of principles governing church polity, organization, and programs. Attention is also given to the need for training and growth and all that pertains to the Christian calling.

God has supplied each congregation with the resources necessary to accomplish what He expects of it. He has given each member spiritual gifts as well as natural abilities. These are to be used for the profit of all members and for the world. These resources must be challenged for use to glorify God in the Gospel cause.

The objectives of the program might be stated this way:

1. To extend the kingdom of God in accordance with the divine mandate of its Head, Jesus Christ, to the end that people may be brought to faith in Jesus Christ.

2. To recruit, motivate, nourish, and equip the members, individually or collectively, to carry out this mandate effectively and efficiently by dedication of their total resources.

3. To bear corporate witness to the unity of faith and provide a united defense against false doctrine and schism.

4. To manage and effectively use the diversity of gifts and resources given the church so that they may be used for the common good.

Our Lord Jesus assigned to the congregation functions that are both *internal* and *external:*

1. The *internal program* involves what God expects a congregation to carry on within itself for the benefit of the individual members of the congregation:
   (a) Worship and spiritual life — Christian nurture through Word and Sacrament, and Christian fellowship.
   (b) Christian education — training for growth in faith and knowledge of God for all members.
   (c) Stewardship — Christian growth in service to God and man, equipping members for service.
   (d) Administration of the affairs of the church.
   (e) Shepherding souls — soul-keeping and soul-reclaiming.
   (f) Social welfare — works of Christian charity.[4]

2. The *external program* involves:

    (a) Outreach into the community (evangelism, social welfare)

    (b) Outreach into the country (home missions, welfare agencies)

    (c) Outreach into the whole world (world missions, world relief)

The following diagram is offered to help clarify what has been presented:

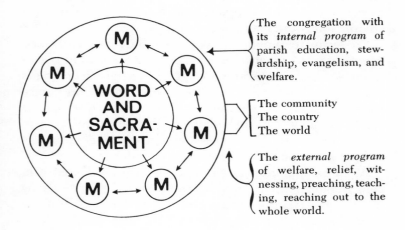

The congregation with its *internal program* of parish education, stewardship, evangelism, and welfare.

The community
The country
The world

The *external program* of welfare, relief, witnessing, preaching, teaching, reaching out to the whole world.

Already in 1914 the great missionary statesman Oswald J. Smith mapped out a definite list of requirements for his church and for his pastorate: "(1) To reach the unsaved for Christ; (2) To turn Christians from worldliness to spirituality; (3) To make the prayer meeting a live service; (4) To build a large enthusiastic Sunday school; (5) To develop a small missionary church; (6) To increase church attendance; (7) To put spiritual men in every office." These challenging goals have brought a great blessing to the People's Church in Toronto, Canada, throughout these years.

Various dangers threaten every congregation: the failure to set worthy objectives which challenge and unify a congregation, lack of a well-rounded program, factionalism, timid pastor or leaders, weak or false doctrine, pride, or complacency. There may be institutional response to crises instead of creative response to goals, strategy designed by a special interest rather than strategy growing from a study process, appraisal by traditional habits rather than by principles and Biblical standards, and members overlooked or underworked rather than members with a reasonable work load.

To evaluate programs, we must study the goals and objectives, note what is being done to work toward reaching these, analyze resources of personnel, discover factors that help or hinder achievement of the goals, and devise ways of remedying weaknesses in the program. Programs should be kept flexible, relate to people, be relevant to a situation, geared for witness and ministry, and be subject to regular and periodic review and reevaluation.

As to developing church programs, we recall that Einstein believed there are easy-to-follow rules underlying this universe. If anybody showed him an involved formula, he would say, "God's laws are simpler than that!"

A very simple approach is what someone has called the "Come and Go" program. "Coming" and "going" are Biblical and essential. This reflects the *gathered* church in worship and the *scattered* church in witness. Come and go: *Come* — to worship, to study the Word, to fellowship, to edify; *go* — to evangelize, to minister and serve the needs of men.

Effective Organization to Serve a Maximum Number of People Effectively

Exodus 18 tells how Moses learned from his father-in-law a good lesson of effective organization to serve the needs of people. Jethro rejoiced over all that the Lord had done for the children of Israel. When he saw that many people stood all day long around Moses, who held court by himself to advise the people, Jethro told him that this was wrong and that he was wearing himself out and that the task was too heavy.

Jethro told Moses that he should be the people's advocate with God and instruct the people generally in the laws and the procedures they were to follow, while honest men, not covetous, should be selected as leaders and advisers of the people. There were to be leaders in divisions of 1,000, of 100, of 50, and of 10. They were to act as judges for the people on all ordinary occasions. All difficult and important cases they could bring to Moses, but all ordinary cases they would judge for themselves. In this way the people would be happy and their problems would be settled effectively.

Some enterprising person made a graph of how Moses may have undertaken his responsibilities. It shows how ineffective an organization Moses really had. Then this person outlined the suggestion which Jethro made to Moses. These graphs give an indelible impression of the importance of delegating tasks in the congregation's program.

The Pastor's Role

The pastor has a very vital function in the church, as he sets the spiritual tone by his ministry of the Word. The pastor is a gift of Christ to the church. He enables the people to perform their ministry, and in no way substitutes for them. He must not only know how to interpret the Bible, but also how to interpret man and counsel him with clear Biblical insight.[5]

God feeds and provides the spiritual flock through pastors and leaders to exercise the ministry of the Word. They are to undergird, sustain, and comfort the people committed to their care. Above all, they should be Spirit-

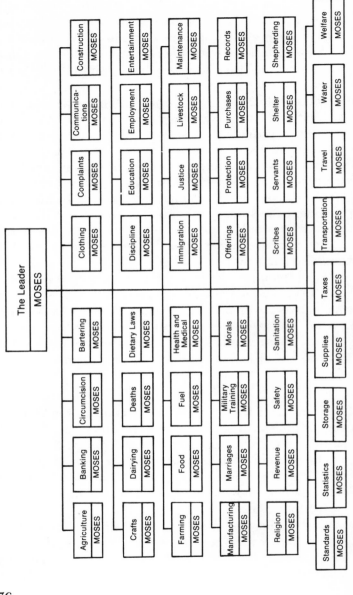

The Leader
MOSES

Box	Head
Agriculture	MOSES
Banking	MOSES
Circumcision	MOSES
Bartering	MOSES
Clothing	MOSES
Complaints	MOSES
Communications	MOSES
Construction	MOSES
Crafts	MOSES
Dairying	MOSES
Deaths	MOSES
Dietary Laws	MOSES
Discipline	MOSES
Education	MOSES
Employment	MOSES
Entertainment	MOSES
Farming	MOSES
Food	MOSES
Fuel	MOSES
Health and Medical	MOSES
Immigration	MOSES
Justice	MOSES
Livestock	MOSES
Maintenance	MOSES
Manufacturing	MOSES
Marriages	MOSES
Military Training	MOSES
Morals	MOSES
Offerings	MOSES
Protection	MOSES
Purchases	MOSES
Records	MOSES
Religion	MOSES
Revenue	MOSES
Safety	MOSES
Sanitation	MOSES
Scribes	MOSES
Servants	MOSES
Shelter	MOSES
Shepherding	MOSES
Standards	MOSES
Statistics	MOSES
Storage	MOSES
Supplies	MOSES
Taxes	MOSES
Transportation	MOSES
Travel	MOSES
Water	MOSES
Welfare	MOSES

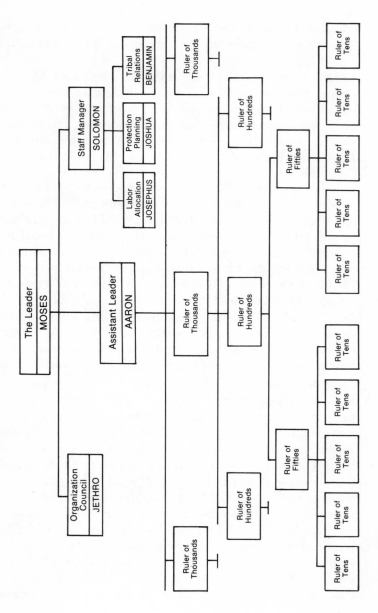

The Leader
MOSES

Organization Council
JETHRO

Staff Manager
SOLOMON

Labor Allocation
JOSEPHUS

Protection Planning
JOSHUA

Tribal Relations
BENJAMIN

Assistant Leader
AARON

Ruler of Thousands

Ruler of Thousands

Ruler of Thousands

Ruler of Hundreds

Ruler of Hundreds

Ruler of Hundreds

Ruler of Fifties

Ruler of Fifties

Ruler of Tens

Ruler of Tens

Ruler of Tens

Ruler of Tens

Ruler of Tens

Ruler of Tens

Ruler of Tens

Ruler of Tens

Ruler of Tens

Ruler of Tens

led, have a holy boldness and a divine tenderness in using their trained knowledge and skills for the proclamation of the Gospel.

The pastor should have a proper image of himself. Samuel Blizzard's survey of the average Protestant minister's image of his roles revealed this sequence: (1) preacher, (2) pastor, (3) organizer, (4) administrator, (5) teacher. Ranked according to *time* actually used in his ministry: (1) administrator, (2) pastor, (3) preacher, (4) organizer, (5) teacher.[6]

It is noteworthy that the pastor seems to be forced to be administrator, first of all, and that both in his image and time used he is last of all a teacher. Preaching and teaching should not be so radically separated in a pastor's mind and in his work, either in regard to their relative importance or in regard to their mutual implications for each other.

"What Do Pulpit Giants Have in Common?" was the question raised in an April 8 and June 17, 1970, article in *The Herald.* Donald E. Demaray made the following observations, which should be stimulating reading for pastors in their self-evaluation: All preach the Scriptures with power. The call to preach is taken with utmost seriousness. They are possessed with a passion to communicate. All have, sooner or later, a crisis of self-realization, a spiritual struggle. All understand the human heart. They are eager students with an insatiable desire to read and gather information. Teaching is found in the preacher's communication pattern. They are fervent evangelists, for they want to see people converted. While all tend to have their own emphases, the whole Gospel—judgment and grace—is preached. They have the capacity to catch the mood and needs of their time. They tend to be fulfilled men. Simplicity characterizes their preaching (not simplistic, but simple). They have a burning within their souls to see renewal. They know continuing religious experiences. Their preaching is exegetical, prophetic, and liturgical.

They are faithful — never neglecting the call of duty, they go beyond it. All are characterized by great joy. They are highly sensitive men.

The work of the church will be strengthened by leaders who go forth in Christ's name courageously. John Heuss suggests: "No parish can fulfill its true function unless there is at the very center of its leadership a small community of quietly fanatic, changed, and truly converted Christians. We want quiet fanatics, men who will outlive and outsuffer the worst sufferings . . . and within their little community reveal to others a kind of Christian relationship that is so different and so accepting that it cannot be resisted. . . . Whenever any parish can create at the center of its leadership life a similar small and truly different nexus of relationships, then nothing can stop the church from realizing its true function." [7]

Notes to Chapter 6

¹ John 10:27-30; Rom. 9:24-26; Eph. 1:4-12; 2:12-13; 5:26-32; Col. 1:18; 2 Tim. 1:9-10; Heb. 4:14; 1 Peter 2:9; 5:2-4.

² Matt. 28:18-20; Rom. 12:6-8; 1 Cor. 12:4-11; 2 Cor. 5:19; Eph. 4: 11-12.

³ John Heuss, *Our Christian Vocation* (Greenwich, Conn.: Seabury Press, 1955).

⁴ John 8:31-32; Rom. 12; 1 Cor. 9:19-22; 12; 2 Cor. 12:19; Eph. 4.

⁵ Eph. 4:1-16.

⁶ "The Training of the Parish Pastor," *Union Seminary Quarterly Review*, XI, 2 (January 1966), 47.

⁷ John Heuss, *Our Christian Vocation* (Greenwich, Conn.: Seabury Press, 1955).

Chapter 7

Educate to Make Disciples

The church really has two great commissions: to evangelize and to educate. The Great Commission requires the church to "teach them to observe all things whatsoever I have commanded you" (Matt. 28:19-20). Christian education is that process of teaching, training, and evangelization by which the individual Christian is nurtured toward maturing in Christian knowledge and faith. It results in attitudes and actions that reflect a growing Christian understanding and experience of Christian service.

Christian education should make disciples, preparing people for their radical tasks in the world, for only the Word of God empowers people to do the work of God. Congregations cannot claim faithfulness to the Great Commission if they neglect the spiritual nurture of the members for their daily lives.

High priority was given to the training of members and lay leaders in the early church, as they met together regularly to study the Word of God. St. Paul had a training program in Corinth for two lay people, Aquila and Priscilla his wife, who later "expounded . . . the way of God more perfectly" to Apollos, who in turn became a preacher of the Word and a defender of faith who "mightily convinced the Jews, and that publicly, showing by the Scriptures that Jesus was Christ" (Acts 18:1-3, 26, 28).

Paul initiated a Bible-training program for lay leaders in Ephesus to establish a deeper spiritual church, so that "all they which dwelt in Asia heard the Word of the Lord Jesus, both Jews and Greeks" (Acts 19:10). They trained their lay leaders at Ephesus at great personal cost "with many tears . . . and kept back nothing that was profitable. . . . By the space of three years I ceased not to warn everyone

night and day with tears" (Acts 20:19-20, 31). He emphasized thorough training of lay leaders when he said to
Timothy: "The things that thou hast heard of me among
many witnesses, the same commit thou to faithful men,
who shall be able to teach others also" (2 Tim. 2:2).

Objectives and Goals

An objective of Christian education is to satisfy the
spiritual hunger of each Christian and to help him develop
intellectually (mind), emotionally (heart), and volitionally
(will) as a disciple of Christ. The objective is development
of abilities, attitudes, and habits. To put it another way, we
want an ever-increasing enlightenment of the mind, renewal of the heart, and eagerness to do good works.

Equipping the saints through Christian training seeks
to provide moral and ethical reinforcement for critical
choices and decisions to be made in life. It produces an
awareness of God and the need for personal salvation, and
a true concern for others.

The goals of total Christian education are to teach God's
infallibly inspired written Word, the Bible; to present
Jesus Christ as Savior and Lord of every person; to relate
God's Word to life in relevant application; to inspire, train,
and provide spiritual motivation for leaders to be effective
in edifying others; and to build the church of the Lord
Jesus Christ, leading youth and adults to a growing relationship with Him.

Christian education should make for a trained and
disciplined mind that never settles for anything less than
God's goals for one's life, governed by a Christian spirit
of integrity, inspired by a personal relationship with the
living Christ, and motivated by a burning desire to be
Christ's person to help make a troubled world whole again.
The educational challenge is to proclaim the Gospel and
God's Word in such a way that people can hear it and,

enlightened by the Holy Spirit, accept it, respond to it, and be transformed by God's grace.

Effective and persuasive teaching of the Word motivates and enlightens, informs and equips Christ's people for their radical ministry on earth.

Adequate Curriculum

The curriculum should provide Biblical studies that constantly involve learning of man's relationship with God, and then between man and man. The curriculum involves the presentation of saving truth, which is consistent with the total Word of God to provide a perspective for an integrated life.

The curriculum should provide adequate information and lead to relevant Biblical understanding and experiences in:

1. Comprehending the natural world as a universe created by God with laws and powers that are to be learned and used as a gift of God to man, for which man is a manager and accountable to God;

2. Living in human societies to express the new man, that is, a Christ-life consistent with the power and love experienced in the new birth by God's grace through faith;

3. Growing personal relationships, working in families and groups to enrich fellowmen for witness to the Gospel of Jesus Christ;

4. Understanding and using one's daily work as a ready service to fellowmen, living for purposes greater than one's self-interest;

5. Effecting the lives of all people on earth by evangelizing and missionizing so that everyone may "hear the voice of the Lord and know Him by faith."

Educational materials are to allow God's Word to be heard with integrity in its own context without negative interpretations. They should speak with assurance of God's miraculous power and goodness then and now, as the Scriptures are taught to emphasize such eternal values as will help people solve their problems today. Learners are to be encouraged to commit themselves fully to Jesus Christ as their personal Savior and Lord, and to have a right relationship with God as a necessary precondition for having right relationships with their fellowmen.

Parents are to be involved through home cooperation in lessons beamed at the children, and in classes which they themselves attend (children and parents learning together for life). Lesson materials as additional resources should be evaluated in terms of the entire Scriptures (Law and Gospel), related to living in today's world and current issues. Teachers should be willing to accept ongoing leadership training to gain the necessary skills for effective teaching.

If the radical nature of Christianity is to be seen in daily practice, education programs should not present the curious marriage of John Dewey's pragmatism and religious humanism with existentialism, all of which involve relativism and reject the absolute values of God's Word. The eternal truths of the Christian faith are not to be put up for a democratic popular vote. The modern solution — a wrong one — offered in some churches in their curricula is to denigrate the doctrinal and historical content of the Bible and the Creeds.

Sometimes Biblical content has been replaced by "laboratory experiences" in Christian community. This "life laboratory" of the new curriculum, which presents relativism and a "Christ-style" at the same time, can be no substitute for Bible-centered Christian education. Some observers have stated that this has produced a generation of religious illiterates who share their insights in dialog and are graded in terms of relationships in the group and between groups rather than in terms of Biblical knowledge and absolutes. This concept means that there is no final right or wrong, except in terms of deviation from the group, and that students do not fail, only teachers fail. Thus educational agencies become religious sociological laboratories rather than centers of Biblical learning.

The educational curriculum should lead to spiritual progress in understanding and action (Heb. 6:1-3). It should lead to overcoming of the great deficiency of people in spiritual discernment and insights. There can be no enlightened action in the absence of an enlightened church membership. Because too much is taken for granted, the church is filled with hungry people who have been inadequately fed and also with bewildered people who wonder what the church is really all about and who do little more than go through the motions.

Christian education is a ministry of teaching by the church via its day school, Sunday school, part-time agencies, Bible classes, youth and men and women's organizations. It also involves special renewal retreats for officers, where they can get away from the ordinary busy life and meet together in a quiet place to discuss spiritual matters and values.

We believe that the great predicament in the churches is not a shortage of money or of workers but a shortage of training in God's Word, which alone leads to a strong witness to Christ. The basic problems in the churches will be settled in the field of Christian education. Provide a person with understanding and proper tools, and he will likely make a proper response.

We have assumed too much understanding on the part of leaders and members with the result that we have turned to the form and function before people were really ready for action. Someone has said that the *average* church member is about as well equipped to do battle with the world as a boy with a B-B gun or slingshot facing a row of machine guns.

We can learn something from Adolf Hitler's rules of communication in *Mein Kampf*, when he proposed simplicity, repetition, and passion: "Make it simple, say it often, and make it burn." As Christians we should teach with simplicity, authority, and urgency.

The Christian education program should meet directly the criticism of *cheap grace* by Dietrich Bonhoeffer: "The upshot of it all is that my only duty as a Christian is to leave the world for an hour or so on a Sunday morning and go to church to be assured that we are all forgiven by Jesus Christ." [1]

Bethel Bible Series

Harley Swiggum, the founder and director of the Bethel Bible Series, wrote us: "I as one member of the body of believers believe so fervently in the need for Biblical study for adults in the Christian family because as we pursue Biblical study we are confronted directly with the Person Jesus Christ and the presence and the power of the Holy Spirit, and in that confrontation we are remolded into persons who by nature of our faith have a deeper compassion for all of humankind's needs as well as a power and a faith relationship to be used by God in a historical process to minister to those needs."

The Bethel Series uses an approach which some congregations have utilized to good advantage. It has some unique and attractive features. It attempts to acquaint the student with the basic fundamentals of both Old and New Testament narratives by providing an overview of the Biblical message. It provides a base or springboard from which to pursue a depth study of God's Word, accenting the necessity of seeing the various parts of the Biblical message in their direct relationship to the historical context in which that message was given.

The course presupposes and demands academic discipline on the part of its participants. In both teacher-trainee and congregational phases, reading assignments precede each segment of study, and participants are required to do considerable memorization. The presentation leans strongly toward the lecture method.

To aid in the retention of what the student has learned in the study of the Bible itself, the program makes use of a series of 40 paintings, which are illustrations or posters that serve to summarize a body of knowledge and which carry specific meanings that have been imposed upon them.

Before the Bethel Series can be used in a congregation, the pastor, education director, or other designated staff member must attend a two-week training in Madison, Wis.

The Home and Family — a Center for Bible Study

The church is only as strong as its families and homes. The "church in thy house" was a central factor in early New Testament Christianity. Christian education should provide Scriptural direction for the family. One of the outstanding blueprints in God's Word for the Christian home is found in Ephesians (ch. 5), where we learn about: 1. Relationship to God; 2. Walking in love and abstaining from evil; 3. Using time as a gift from God; 4. Seeking the right relationship with the Holy Spirit; 5. Worshiping; 6. Holding father, mother, and children in high regard; 7. Using the Lord's weapons to fight spiritual battles.

The bond to hold the family together is meaningful, loving, and honest dedication to God's Word. If the church and its educational agencies do not bring their influence to bear in making proper spiritual choices and decisions, TV, movies, friends, and other forces will. The family should be recognized for what it is — a place of influence in which the church will call Christians back to action.

Taking Christian communication seriously, the Christian home should be a nurturing center, where a family of Christian priests unites in worship, Bible reading, and prayer.

The congregation should be structured to provide time for the family to develop a unit life. It should not plan its ministry primarily for individuals torn out of the context of the family, but plan to teach and train family units. It is important to view the family as the focal point of the internal task of the congregation.

If the churches were to reform their programs with the family unit as the focal ministry, they would consider these elements:

1. Responsibility for nurture and outreach would be shifted from the church to the family.

2. Responsibility for outreach would be accepted by the family and family units, instead of by a few individuals being sent out from the church building.

3. Family units would be given support as units. This would mean that there would be more preaching about the Christian home, programs with families in mind, more preparing of helpful materials for families, and avoidance of monopolizing the family's time.

A Conditioning Program

The Christian education program is a conditioning program for one's spiritual life. Some years ago, when the first astronauts were sent to orbit the moon and come back to earth, a TV commentator was interviewing one of the astronaut's wives. He commented about the bravery and courage of these men to be committed to the round-trip flight to the moon despite its many possibilities for error and defeat. The commentator asserted that in his opinion this was the greatest example of bravery and courage in the history of the world, greater than Columbus' sailing to America, etc. The astronaut's wife commented that she did not think that this feat involved such great bravery or courage at this moment because they had been *conditioned* for the experience, having gone through much practice and simulation. If we had been in the flight capsule, we would have gone into shock because we would not have been physically, emotionally, or psychologically prepared. A person has to be conditioned for such an experience.

There is a point here to be learned in the church: If today we went to 60% of the homes of most congregations and would tell the people that they should come with us to make an evangelism or mission call and do all the talking, they would go into shock and point to the impossibility of their doing it. The reason for shock would be that the church has not conditioned them for such witnessing and evangelism.

Another example: If we went to 60% of the homes of congregations to tell them to begin tithing tomorrow, giving 10% of their income to the Lord, they would say that it cannot be done. Though the challenge is not unreasonable, yet they would go into shock because they are not conditioned or trained for such a response to the Lord.

Most people have not been properly prepared for life. Christian education programs are the conditioning of members for living faithfully for their Savior. As physical conditioning through exercise provides physical and mental vigor, so spiritual training through education in God's Word provides spiritual vigor and vitality. The reason why many people have spiritual "borderline anemia" is that the church has not involved them in a vital educational process that guides them into Scriptural truth. Young Timothy would not have known the Holy Scriptures except that from a child he was effectively taught them.

Christian education will provide training in a climate where every learner may gain a strong faith in Jesus. Such conditioning involves the unquestioning acceptance of God's Word and the questioning of a Word-less life and humanistic values. It includes loving instruction, patient nurture, prayer, and an exciting discovery of God's truth.

Notes to Chapter 7

¹ Dietrich Bonhoeffer, *The Cost of Discipleship* (New York: Macmillan, 1960), p. 3.

Chapter 8

Speak the Word of Edify and to Help Each Other (Fellowship)

God calls His people to share His edifying Word for mutual encouragement. Each Christian has a responsibility for the faith and life of others. Each must work together with each other one in the body of Christ as a nurturing and fruitful members. Christians bring the Word of God to bear on each other for mutual growth whenever they gather for worship and teaching. Studying God's Word together, joining in prayer and singing, edifies people as each one does so for the sake of the other.[1]

A major purpose of the edifying Word among Christians is not only to build up faith, but also to mend what has been torn down, to remedy false teaching, to remove suspicions and divisions, to counteract prejudice, or to neutralize the damage of division. This is God's unique and radical way of moving all Christians into an active relationship to each other so that they are always mutually helpful in all situations. All of this activity is the work of Jesus Christ and the Holy Spirit, who wants us all to "attain to the unity of the faith and of the knowledge of the Son of God, to mature manhood, to the measure of the stature of the fulness of Christ; so that we may no longer be children, tossed to and fro and carried about with every wind of doctrine. . . . Rather, speaking the truth in love, we are to grow up in every way into Him who is the Head, into Christ, from whom the whole body . . . makes bodily growth and up-builds itself in love" (Eph. 4:13-16, RSV).[2]

Among all the helpful things we do for each other is to help each other remember that Jesus Christ, the Son of God, has redeemed us and is our Lord. This dynamic

Word is not simply some equipment we use, but it is a radical force that ignites us and puts us to work in all of the tasks and purposes for which God's children live in the world.[3]

Koinonia

It sometimes seems to be a weak procedure to use words, but the Word is the power of God to give mutual encouragement. This power is dynamic in us when we hear and read the sacred Scriptures. The basic idea in edifying is a radical one, as Christians are to share their time, their faith, their personalities, and other gifts with each other. The Greek word for fellowship in the New Testament — *koinonia* — occurs 39 times. It is a lively thing, telling us that what is happening among those involved is something good. Every problem, fear, or worry is to be fellowshiped because Christians care about each other. This could be called close partnership or companionship, which implies mutual concern and mutual action. By God's grace we have become partners together with our Lord Jesus Christ.[4]

The New Testament tells of this *koinonia* as a togetherness to share, to participate together, with Jesus in the center. This it is that makes it the church and not just another organization. It is the purpose of the Holy Spirit to give power in unity as He creates lively fellowship among people of diverse racial, cultural, and social backgrounds. It might be called the "circle of the concerned," with Jesus Christ as Leader.

Christians are a community that possesses a unique spiritual solidarity and interdependence. As the organs in the body must hold and live together or die, so the individual Christian can only live in close relationship with Christ and with other members of the church.[5]

A church will assume various forms on earth, which should allow it to be very active, very maneuverable, not passive. The power proceeding from the Word actually

92

shapes this into a productive fellowship. The fellowshiping and working community is the community awakened and supported by the Word of grace.

Fellowship is designed to keep and strengthen Christians, to lead sinners to repentance, and to discipline the erring. Thus the fellowship group proceeds from the Word and leads back to the Word.

Small Group Fellowship — Cell Groups

Since Christian faith is to be shared, opportunities should be provided in small groups to discover the purpose and meaning of life. Christian fellowship is not only a vertical relationship, that is, a sharing in and with Christ, but also a horizontal relationship — the sharing together of Christians between each other in and with Christ.

Cell groups of Christians fellowshiping together date back to the first century, for it was largely through the activities of little groups or cells of believers that the message of Jesus Christ spread throughout the Roman Empire. Their purpose is to prepare the Christians to function as witnessing groups in the midst of society, to help all members gain the right attitudes, and to make the right decisions for Christian influence in the world.

Through meeting regularly the early disciples gained a new vision and acquired a new understanding of the meaning of world history — His story. Even though they were a despised minority, they possessed a burning hope for the future and a great confidence in ultimate times of change.

Basic characteristics of cell groups of believers are that they exist for the training of the members and emphasize the necessity for a renewed mind. Paul called on the Christians to be transformed by the renewing of the mind, to have the mind of Jesus Christ: "Let the Word of Christ dwell in you richly in all wisdom" (Col. 3:16). They are to be vitally concerned with the relationships and hap-

93

penings of daily life, discussing the application of faith to the details of everyday situations.

Before a Christian cell group can be formed, several people are to be given a clear grasp of the objectives and an understanding of the need for a disciplined plan for fellowship. Members are asked to accent the following responsibilities: 1. Spend some time alone with God every day in meditation. 2. Set aside a definite time each week to meet with each other in a gathering and study of God's Word and prayer. 3. Undertake Bible study in order to equip themselves for more effective witness. 4. Engage in personal evangelism. 5. Be active in the church, recognizing their responsibility to give regularly of their ability and money to the work of the Lord.

Cell groups have no right to exist unless they are firmly rooted in the local churches in whose name they act. They cannot act as societies apart from, or superior to, the local church. The group exists as a training school in Christian discipleship, driving people to reexamine their personal attitudes, and to a continual rediscovery of the explosive power of the Gospel, resulting in a growing faith and stronger commitment to Christ.

The group meetings might be divided into four areas: 1. Bible study. 2. Sharing of experiences. 3. Prayer. 4. Social opportunity. There should be sharing of spiritual insights through probing discussions.

Koinonia should always be explosive or radical, driving one deeper into the church of the Lord Jesus Christ, and then driving one out into the world to fulfill the mission of the church. This is so important because the church is crowded with nominal members, scarcely aware of the new life in Christ which the Scriptures offer to, and demand of, all disciples of Christ.

As Jesus invested Himself and His time in 12 men, and poured His life into theirs, strengthening their lives by sharing the Word of the Father, so cell groups are designed to have Christ shared from the lips and lives of each other for the good of all. If we all belong to Christ, we belong to each other.

The church needs to be reminded that teaching takes place not only in Sunday school or Bible class but also in groups. Thus the entire church is unified, as the pastor or a designated leader of the congregation meets with one person representing each group in an "action group council" in preparation for the weekly meetings of the individual groups.

The strength of the church will be best judged not by the number attending the meetings but by the number of additional vital, active groups formed by experienced members. All this is to help one another live as people moved by Christ (1 Peter 4:1-11). "They devoted themselves to the apostles' teaching and fellowship" (Acts 2:42).

Next to the sermon and pastoral calls, only the personal contact of member to member will be adequate in making a total spiritual impact on each individual. This personal contact through groups in home visitations or group meetings, where five to seven families are involved, meets the following needs: people get better acquainted with each other; vital fellowship among members is provided; inactive and delinquent people are aided; new members are properly integrated; people are informed and gain necessary information.

The plan may include the following:

1. Group meetings or visitation into all homes (vary the approach) on spiritual matters at least three times a year.

2. The congregation is divided into convenient geographic districts (20 to 30 families in one area), whose leader is an elder or deacon with two or three assistants (depending upon how many families are in the area). Make a card file of families according to geographic areas. List visitors in the area they serve.

Mutual Care for Growth and Purity

"Whatever Happened to Church Discipline?" is the challenging article and question by Jay Robertson Mc-Quilkin. Asking, "How important is it for the church to be pure and united?" the author states: "When either the unity or the purity is lost, the body of Christ no longer has a right to expect its ministry to be fruitful. . . . A disunited church or a compromising church not only denies the character of God and loses its testimony to the world, but cannot adequately fulfill God's purpose for its own members."[6]

Underlying church discipline is mutual care under the Law-Gospel word, threat-promise words, judgment-mercy words, which accomplish what God purposes. When defections from God's Word in doctrine and life become evident, this Word is to be used. Dietrich Bonhoeffer said: "Nothing can be more cruel than the tenderness that confines another to his sin. Nothing can be more compassionate than the severe rebuke that calls a brother back from the path of sin."[7]

Mutual care in the church occupies the place which lies between the Word of God and sinful man. Discipline seems to be a lost dimension in most Christian churches. When we included the church discipline of Matthew 18 in a previous book, *Winning Them Back*, we were told by some that churches no longer found this acceptable and that it should not be a part of the book. Whatever happened to church discipline and Matthew 18? It is the use of the radical Word to accomplish radical purposes for people.

When there is a wound in the human body, it corrects and helps itself as aid comes through certain substances and mechanisms to fight the infection so that the wound is healed. The body of Christ should work the same way in interdependence and in carrying out self-corrective "spiritual body action." That's mutual care and discipline.

When someone mentions discipline, many think of punishment for misbehavior, but it actually means a protective structure to aid, strengthen, and correct each other. Mutual care in the church, or the lack of it, must eventually affect the life of all. Christians cannot afford to be indifferent about sin in their own lives or in the lives of fellow members, for when they do not forgive or receive forgiveness, the ties that bind them to Christ and to Christ's people have been torn (1 Cor. 12:12-26).

Edification and church discipline is that love for the brethren which is concerned for each individual's salvation. It is all part of the Gospel, the story of God's love for men. It is shown by communication of the Word, edification, confrontation, encouragement, admonition, and prayer.

God has commanded mutual care such as this, and the welfare of the church demands it. Christ's procedure for exercising love through evangelical discipline in the church is outlined in Matthew 18:15-20. The offender is to be told his fault privately in order to have an opportunity to repent and change. If this is fruitless, the earnest efforts of one or two witnesses, besides the brother who first sought to show love and help, should be made. Finally, the special love, prayers, and admonition of the entire congregation should be sought to warn the erring brother, befriend him, and to rescue him from the dangerous consequences of adherence to his sins. If he still does not change, he must be dealt with decisively.[8]

The primary purpose of discipline is to save or restore the person who has sinned. Discipline is a sign and evidence of love, not of destruction. The purpose is to correct the fault, to restore the offender, to preserve the good testimony of the church, and to protect other members from falling into the same error. Another reason for it is to keep the church pure, as Christ intended.[9]

When a member is guilty of a fault of such a nature that it affects the Biblical testimony and standard which the church is endeavoring to maintain, there should be evangelical discipline.

As there is a mutual agreement in the confession and testimony of the church, there is to be mutual caring and also binding and freeing of sins. The Scriptural origin and basis for authority in church discipline is to be found in the commission of our Lord: "I will give unto thee the keys of the kingdom of heaven, and whatsoever thou shalt bind on earth shall be bound in heaven, and whatsoever thou shalt loose on earth shall be loosed in heaven" (Matt. 16:19). The scope of this authority is indicated by the rather stark expressions of "binding" and "loosing."

The church (the assembly of Christian people gathered around the means of grace in a locality) has been delegated by God to pronounce absolution on the penitent sinner, and embrace in faith the forgiveness procured for him through Christ's sacrifice on the cross. This is the "key" that opens the gate of heaven to the believer. At the same time, the congregation has been empowered to close or "bind" the heavenly portals to the impenitent sinner. Jesus told the disciples on the first Easter evening: "Receive ye the Holy Ghost; whosesoever sins ye remit, they are remitted unto them; and whosesoever sins ye retain, they are retained." [10]

Whether we admonish or comfort, encourage or seriously reprimand, we offer the proclamation of the judgment and mercy of God in Christ Jesus. It is an awesome thing that the church has been empowered with the radical, negative function of administering church discipline, of "excluding manifest and impenitent sinners from the Christian congregation." [11]

Exercising its authority under Christ, the church, however, never acts in an authoritarian way, but only in tune with Scriptural authority. Authoritarionism is always an extraneous thing, relying on position, prestige, power, and the organizational and professional stance. The Christian community is given this authority to establish ordinances and to observe them as a response to God's Word, and these are incorporated in a constitution and a confession. This requires the church to watch over the work of its pastors, leaders, and to seek the well-being of every individual member.

Dead wrong is a view of God and man which assumes that an approach of mutual care and evangelical discipline alienates people or is destructive of fellowship. Churches will not want to keep the peace at any price, at the price of denying principle, at the price of letting people destroy themselves by not repenting of their sins. Without discipline and without mutual restraints, we would all become savages, at the mercy of one another's desires and appetites.

No family, no society, and no church can be preserved in a proper condition without discipline, which forms one of the ligaments that bind the members together and hold each one in its proper place. Discipline serves as a curb and restraint for those who disobey the Word of God and as a spur to stimulate the inactive. But discipline never makes its regulations more important than people.

People have two basic needs: love and discipline. Discipline without love is tyranny; love without discipline is pure sentimentality and may develop into harmful license or "doing one's own thing." Discipline must always be an expression of the church's testimony and belief. It recognizes standards as essential to the ordering of the church's life.

Attitudes necessary in mutual caring and evangelical discipline are: faith, objectivity, humility, candid self-evaluation, openness, honesty, commitment, passionate conviction to share God's Word, and earnest concern for the salvation of all men.

Self-discipline is the best kind of discipline, as the new man puts down the old man and his evil habits by Christ through the Word. Such self-discipline means daily repentance for one's sins, confession of sins to God, confession of sins to fellowmen, forgiveness of sins through renewal of faith in Jesus Christ by the Gospel, and renewing by the Spirit. Thus the child of God remains under the control of God the Holy Spirit by the means of grace, for Christ is in control of his life. That's the disciplined life.[12]

Biblical Fellowship Principles

Mutual care among Christians also happens between congregations, which calls for fellowship between churches. Christian unity and fellowship between churches is a requirement of our Lord. The church is to have one Spirit, one hope, one Lord, one faith, one baptism, one God. The sphere of one Lord and one faith transcends all outward structures. The unity of the church is promoted by the teaching of the Gospel and of God's infallible Word.[13]

The existence of the one church *as churches*, extended over time and space, is not by itself a contradiction of the church's essential unity. Fragmentary or sectarian denominational emphases which move away from a clear Scriptural basis cause churches to give imperfect or distorted witness to the Gospel and create obstacles to the true unity of the church. Churches whose separate existence is grounded in basic theological differences of faith and order should not ignore these differences but should seek to resolve them by recognizing such differences and by correcting them according to the clear teaching of the Scriptures.

The first great division in the church today is a division within denominations and within congregations—a tragic situation. The demand for a "diversity within unity" position, which means that opposing doctrines may coexist, creates a split which hampers effective unity for Gospel outreach.

An appearance of unity and a practice of fellowship

based on anything else than clear Scripture or which ignores pure doctrine of Scripture is harmful. Unity must never be put first, for fellowship follows agreement in doctrine.

There is a strong tendency toward fellowship on the basis of a "least common denominator." If fragmentation is costly, external uniformity or organization that overlooks doctrinal differences is even more costly. Uniting churches organizationally does not make it easier for people to believe in Christ or accept the truth of God's Word.

Ecumenical circles often speak today about a theological consensus (synthesis) as the key to Christian unity. This actually has a divisive effect on Christians, rather than uniting them. To say that we agree on more doctrines than we disagree on is simplistic and Scripturally unreal. The consensus theory, instead of being the key to unity, actually unlocks the floodgates of human speculations about Christian doctrine and encourages bickering and endless arguing.

The contemporary ecumenical crisis comes from a misunderstanding of the church by improperly externalizing the nature of the church and by forgetting that the church is *invisible* and is *one*. Inadequate bases for church fellowship include denial of the possibility of correct doctrinal formulations, advocacy of pluralistic doctrinal positions, equating denominational fellowship with Christian unity, limiting the extent of doctrinal agreement, and minimizing the importance of the faithful practice of God's Word. False ecumenism wants organizational unity instead of Scriptural unity.

Even though denominational differences are very serious and regrettable, they are not the scandal of Christianity as much as is the belittling of the great Christian doctrines and of the authority and integrity of the written Scriptures. The scandal of Christendom is the tragic lack of conviction on the part of those who substitute outward organization for true spiritual oneness in God's Word. Often the "united front" of ecumenical activity is not on Biblical truth but on the name and influence of the church for a broad "Christian" philosophy in social affairs.

Henri Blocher in "The Nature of Biblical Unity," a paper read at the Lausanne 1974 World Congress, stated that doctrinal pluralism and diversity within churches is "contraband goods which they want to hide by flying the New Testament flag. . . . The possibilities of expressing Christian unity are proportional to the doctrinal agreement reached. The fellowship and cooperation which express unity have various stages and form. They can be institutional, permanent, frequent, occasional, exceptional; in worship, evangelism, teaching, social work. Two ministers can feed the same flock, or join on the same platform to protest against pornography. I suggest that we draw several concentric circles on a paper. The inside circle could be the one where Paul met the Philippians (Phil. 3:15); others would correspond to a less complete agreement that would permit only looser associations." He added, "Christians ought to consider abnormal their differences in matters of faith, even secondary ones. . . ."

Unscriptural fellowship with other churches involves toleration of error whether by formal agreement to differ or by passive consent. It occurs when two parties not in doctrinal agreement grant each other the right to entertain and to teach their views even though one view is unscriptural, when they agree not to criticize each other's views or to charge each other with teaching error, when they declare a false doctrine as nondivisive although it conflicts with a doctrine clearly revealed in Scripture, when they engage in joint religious acts which normally express agreement in faith although they have not resolved to have fellowship with each other. They are not only to subscribe to their doctrine, but also to proclaim it and to practice it faithfully. Unscriptural fellowship means acceptance of differences in doctrine, which are ignored by conducting joint religious acts and worship.

By God's grace congregations and church bodies are to be "of one heart and of one soul," "of one mind," "all speak the same thing . . . perfectly joined together in the same mind and in the same judgment," having "one faith," "one spirit, with one mind striving together for the faith of the Gospel." [14]

Notes to Chapter 8

[1] 1 Cor. 12:12-27; 14:26; Eph. 4:12-13; Col. 3:12-17; Heb. 10:19-25.

[2] Acts 9:22-31; 1 Cor. 12:25; Eph. 2:13-18.

[3] Rom. 1:16; Col. 3:12-17.

[4] 1 Cor. 1:18; 1 Thess. 2:13; 2 Tim. 3:14-17.

[5] Rom. 1:4; 1 Cor. 12:12-31; Eph. 1:22-23; 4:16; Col. 1:18.

[6] Jay Robertson McQuilkin, *Christianity Today*, XVIII, 13 (March 29, 1974), 724 ff.

[7] Dietrich Bonhoeffer, *Life Together* (New York: Harper & Brothers, 1954) pp. 105 ff.

[8] Luke 17:3; 2 Thess. 3:6, 14-15; 1 Tim. 5:20.

[9] Matt. 6:14-25; 1 Cor. 5:5-7; 2 Cor. 7:8-9; Gal. 6:1; 2 Thess. 3:13-15; 1 Tim. 1:19-20; 3:7; Titus 1:1-3.

[10] John 20:22-23; 1 Cor. 5:4-5; 2 Cor. 2:7-10.

[11] Luther's *Small Catechism*, "The Office of the Keys and Confession"; Matt. 18:17; 1 Tim. 1:20; Titus 3:10-11.

[12] Ps. 51:17; Acts 17:11; Gal. 5:24; Eph. 4:23-24; Heb. 12:2; James 5:16; 1 John 1:8-9.

[13] 1 Cor. 12:12-13; Eph. 4:4-6.

[14] Acts 4:31-33; 1 Cor. 1:10; 2 Cor. 13:11; Eph. 4:5; Phil. 1:27.

Chapter 9

Faithful Managers of Resources God Has Given

The stewardship life is related to the stewardship of the Gospel. Unless we see Christian stewardship as a witness to our faith, we shall easily fall prey to activistic and naturalistic programs in order to gain service and money from church members — rendered as a matter of duty rather than as a response to God's grace and love. Christian stewardship involves a supernatural or radical dimension, not merely natural powers. Christian stewardship is doing what comes supernaturally through the growth and development of Christian faith.

Ephesians 2:10 tells us that "we are God's workmanship, created in Christ Jesus unto good works." By God's grace and power man is called to service, enabled, empowered, and given the ability to give. God's plan of grace makes a personal claim on each believer and becomes the determining factor in a continuing response as he is enabled by the Word of God to serve and give as God's manager.[1]

Churches therefore need to present a clear picture of how the Christian grows in stewardship as they continually hold before each church member the "plan that God has for him, God's judgment on his progress or failure in meeting the plan, and God's grace in Christ by which he is enabled to fulfill the plan." [2] The goal of stewardship is to help people move in the direction God wants them to go, challenging the whole person by sharing the whole counsel of God rather than aiming at partial or organizational goals.

God's gifts determine what the tasks of the Christian shall be. He has made adequate provision for doing His work by giving the abilities and money to His people to perform His tasks. Therefore it is the Christian's responsibility to "hold in trust" and to use the talents and possessions which God has lent to him as a manager for Him. The only question is whether he will use them as God intends. God will not ask anyone to do or give anything which He has not first given him. He says, "As every man hath received the gift, so give" (1 Peter 4:10-11). First the gift, then the response.

The vine-branch picture of John 15 shows God as the supernatural source for stewardship action. Christ is the Vine, whose function it is to give life, to produce fruit through the branch. The branch is the Christian, whose function it is to receive the life of the Vine, to bear the fruit of the Vine and for the Vine. No branch can produce fruit by itself. Without the Vine, the branch is dead and powerless, for "without Me," Jesus says, "you can do nothing." Thus God has grafted the believer into Christ, and He makes this a productive union and communion. That is the unique, divine dimension.

Motivation — the Power for Management of Life

The only real motivation for the stewardship life is the grace of God and the love of our Lord Jesus Christ for us. Nothing else. Stewardship motivation is not based on logic, emotion, duty, or needs. Christ loved us and gave Himself for us, for the forgiveness of sins and for life in Him and for Him. The Gospel is the one and the same power to rescue from sin and produce fruits of faith.[3]

We need to recognize that there are various motives and philosophies to which men are tempted to adhere:

1. "Take" philosophy: Personal indulgence and satisfaction (their god is their belly) is the center and motive. It is surrounded by appetite, liquor, sex and lust, ease, narcotics, etc.

2. Pagan philosophy: False will is the center and motive. It is surrounded by idolatry, pride of self or class, search for pleasure, arrogance, exploitation.

3. Main Street (business self-interest) philosophy: Self and greed are the center and motive. They are surrounded by money, possessions, power, culture, pride, social position, etc.

4. Christian philosophy: Christ's love is the center and motive. It is surrounded by faith, mutual trust, generosity, edification, mutual concern, etc.

Christian motivation involves and includes all considerations of the old man-new man tension and the Law-Gospel use, as developed earlier in this book. Only as such motivation is known and accepted will people have the strength to follow God's plan of stewardship.

Objectives and Goals

Stewardship is a matter of religious response, restructuring attitudes and opinions regarding the Christian's involvement in and commitment to the Lord's work—thus a matter of changing behavior. False notions and misunderstandings about Christian giving must be destroyed and be replaced with standards and habits which come from God's Word.

As fellow Christians, bound together as a church, we seek to enrich each one's relationship with God and the quality of his spiritual life. We seek to sharpen a conscience that is responsive to Christ's call and the development of a sense of personal responsibility for reaching more people with the Gospel.

Stewardship commitment, then, involves a long-term educational process, with each year's results accumulatively higher than those before until the full potential has been reached—as God blesses.

Stewardship goals include increased giving as a by-product or secondary result of spiritual renewal and growth in response to Scriptural norms and standards. We will counsel each individual member to make an annual appraisal of his commitment and cultivate him for spiritual development year by year. Christian growth as a goal is here understood in terms of the member's giving in proportion to the gifts God has given him, specifically in terms of a generous percentage and firstfruits.

Total stewardship involves the stewardship of the Gospel. It begins with education in the principles and practices of the Christian stewardship life. This program will enlist and train people for ministry and mission within the church and teach the priesthood of all believers and the Christian calling. It will provide information about Christ's Gospel mission through the church. It will train for the proper use of material resources and wise money management. This program will train the membership in the grace of Christian giving, both of income and accumulated possessions, for Christ and His church.

Two Different Approaches

There are two different approaches we as Christian stewards can take to stewardship: One as beggars; the other, as proclaimers of God's Word. One as promoters; the other, as educators.

The *first approach,* that of begging and promoting, stresses performance and results; it finds dollars as the main product and spiritual growth as a by-product. It carries with it subtle legalisms and much rationalizing.

The *second approach*—an educational one—stresses relationships, growth in faith, fruit, and has dollars as a by-product. This approach is based on the fact that a man will not give properly until he adequately understands (1) his relationship to God; (2) his relationship to his material possessions; and (3) his relationship to his fellowmen. Before he is asked to commit himself, there should be an adequate presentation so that he can understand and be prepared to respond to the challenge of God.

Many congregations find themselves begging and promoting and ought to change to the educational approach. This means they need to:

(1) Change *from* stewardship education aimed at increase in contributions *to* education for all ages to enrich the relationship with God and the quality of people's spiritual life;

(2) Change *from* Christian stewardship limited to church activities *to* a broader concept, which involves all of one's personal, civic, vocational, and political activities;

(3) Change *from* a concern with dollars and service for the church *to* a growing discipleship;

(4) Change *from* dependence on offerings and response to pressure *to* orderly planning and budgeting of resources;

(5) Change *from* church offerings to meet the congregation's bills *to* the offertory as worship, where each person brings his life and substance to the altar;

(6) Change *from* the every-member stewardship visit for pledges *to* every-member commitment on the basis of careful indoctrination in Biblical principles;

(7) Change *from* personal giving measured by mathematical averages *to* giving measured by one's potential participation in ministry and mission;

(8) Change *from* an exclusive emphasis on giving *to* stewardship which also involves earning, spending, saving, investing, and the writing of Christian wills.

The first approach of giving *to needs* is a strictly organizational concept, which presents problems and needs in order to develop a plan to tell people what to give. It will usually provide immediate results and money, but it is a long-range failure.

The second approach of giving *"from* God's blessings" results in a careful study of Biblical concepts and objectives as it takes into consideration current views and resources available, on the basis of which a plan is made to teach and motivate all individuals so that they may be prepared to witness to their faith as a Christian response by God's grace.

Three Requisites for Financial Success

It cannot be too strongly emphasized that the success of stewardship and, specifically giving, must begin with a thorough indoctrination of what the Bible teaches concerning Christian giving. Three considerations are necessary for stewardship success by the Holy Spirit: 1. Law and Gospel oriented messages; 2. Information; 3. A good system.

1. Law and Gospel Oriented Messages

We make a grave mistake if we fail to undergird and surround our stewardship messages to groups and to individuals with the Law and Gospel in all their clarity. The civil war between the old man and the new man is at a high pitch when stewardship and giving are involved. Stewardship failures come from our humanity and sinful flesh, which is estranged from God, and it also comes from the temptation and the deceit of the devil.

The cure for our spiritual sluggishness and stubbornness is first to have our stewardship delinquency and failures exposed by God's law. The Law is not presenting our failure of meeting church budgets (which is man's evaluation of a situation), but a presentation of God's evaluation of man's failure in heeding His holy Word.

Haggai 1 tells how God was displeased in Haggai's day with certain of His people who were living in luxurious homes while His temple was in ruins. They were not concerned about the Lord's work. The result was crop failure and inflation. God said that the inflation and the drought hit them because their only concern was their own good and they ignored His temple and the Lord's work. Was God cold and heartless in doing this? Not at all! For they were destroying themselves in their disregard of Him who created them and their possessions. They had failed to listen to the Word of the Lord, which told them to bring to Him their tithes and offerings in worship of their God. Now God got their attention by holding back their income. He gave them an opportunity to repent and to experience forgiveness to rebuild their relationship to Him.

Malachi 1 tells of another situation when God's people became disobedient to Him by withholding the offerings that God required. At this time the priests or pastors were also guilty. God told them: "A son honors his father, a servant honors his master, I am your Father and Master, yet you don't honor Me, O priests, but you despise My name. 'Who? Us?' you say. 'When did we ever despise Your name?' When you offer polluted sacrifices on My altar. 'Polluted sacrifices? When have we ever done a thing like that?' Every time you say, 'Don't bother bringing anything very valuable to offer to God!' You tell the people, 'Lame animals are all right to offer on the altar of the Lord — yes, even the sick and the blind ones.' And you claim this isn't evil?" (Mal. 1:6-8 Living Bible)

God required the first and the best, but the priests allowed them to bring leftovers, the sick and the crippled. Significantly, God told the priests that they should have shut the doors of the temple and refused people entrance because of their leftover offering. God was not cruel in suggesting this, for He wanted to provide an opportunity for a rude awakening. God was displeased with their worship, for it failed to bring the firstfruits and the best. So we hear God saying: 'Though you have scorned My laws from earliest time, yet you may still return to Me,' says the Lord of Hosts. 'Come and I will forgive you. . . .' Will a man rob

God? Surely not! And yet you have robbed Me. 'What do You mean? When did we ever rob You?' You robbed Me of the tithes and offerings due to Me. And so the awesome curse of God is cursing you, for your whole nation has been robbing Me" (Mal. 3:7-9).

The sad fact is that ever so many in every congregation are apparently robbing God, even while they would not rob a grocery store, a bank, or even their neighbor. Bank robberies get headline notices in newspapers, but every week in every community there are tens of thousands of dollars withheld from God. God calls this "robbery."

God's solution to this problem is the Gospel of forgiveness. When we are cold and freeze, we go to the fire and warm ourselves. When love for the Lord and gifts for His kingdom are cold and sluggish, we should go to the fire of God's love which has been given us in Christ Jesus, for it will warm our hearts to give as God has given to us. God will exchange our poverty for His riches and grace in Christ Jesus: "You know the grace of our Lord Jesus Christ, that though He was rich, yet for your sake He became poor that you through His poverty might be rich" (2 Cor. 8:9). The Gospel is not only a power unto salvation to everyone that believes, but also the power unto sanctification — that causes the offering of one's self and substance to the Lord.

2. *Information*

People give as they know, not as they are able. Instead of taking the time to deal with the real problem — lack of knowledge — we often use the immediate needs of the church and take shortcuts, using secular motives and pressures. Promotional campaigns can never be a substitute for a solid and careful teaching job. Clever fund-raising approaches are not the answer.

Lack of Knowledge

A careful analysis and research in congregations will reveal a great inadequacy in information and knowledge concerning basics of the Biblical standards of giving. During a two-year period the author tested the opinions of the most active members of more than 36 congregations in Wisconsin. The statements of these church members reveal a rather distorted understanding of the Biblical basics of stewardship. The opinions voiced reveal the following:

(1) "I give mainly because I am a member and it is my duty to support the church." About 30% held this opinion contrary to the fact that it is God's love in Christ which should be the main motivation to give.

(2) "I can demonstrate my faith by the percentage I give of my income." About 50% disagreed despite the fact that it is possible to demonstrate a person's faith by the portion of the income he gives to the Lord. "If I had more faith, I would give more." About 50% disagreed with that, even though the Scriptures show the centrality of faith to a person's decision in giving his offerings to the Lord. These answers indicate that almost half of the leading members of these congregations did not understand the centrality of faith and the part that faith plays in generous giving.

(3) "Any efforts to connect Christianity and money is wrong." About 30% of the people believed this is right, which is very disconcerting in view of the fact that the Scriptures from Genesis to Revelation indicate the stewardship responsibility and accountability of all people in regard to all of their possessions, including money. Jesus Christ had much to say about the proper handling of possessions and money. Christianity and money cannot be separated.

(4) "Every member has his fair share of our budget." About 50% believed this is true, but it has never been determined how one decides what the fair share of a congregation's budget really is. What counts is the giving of a fair share of a person's income to God.

(5) "Tradition and custom determine what most members give." About 70% of the people believed this is true, which is a serious indictment because it is God's Word that should determine what members give. This reveals a serious problem which stewardship leaders need to face so that God's will, not tradition and custom, is the determining factor.

(6) "I don't care to talk to another member about the subject of giving." About 45% stated that this was their position. This reluctance ordinarily indicates a lack of understanding and confidence in their own beliefs in the area of giving.

(7) "If we ask people for a commitment in giving, some will leave the church or transfer." About 70% marked this as their opinion, which shows that the majority of the members have a completely negative attitude towards discussion of Christian giving among fellow members and that they are intimidated into believing that the church must keep quiet about the subject or pay the consequences of a negative reaction.

(8) "When all is said and done, people will give about as they always have." About 65% marked "true," which indicates that they don't see much use in having educational programs or every-member stewardship visits. The fact is that effective training programs have been highly successful. The more people are reached effectively, the more have changed their giving habits and have adopted Scriptural standards.

(9) "I don't feel capable of leading others to a higher religious response." About 55% said this was their conviction, which points to a rather sad situation, for all Christians have been called by God to build up the faith of other Christians. What does this say of the attitude of parents in training their children in the way they should go?

(10) "Our family is giving about _____ percent (%) of our yearly income to the Lord:"

No answer—40%   10%—5%
5% or below—36%   11% and above—2%
6—9%—17%

This response indicates a woeful lack of knowledge of Scriptural truths and Biblical standards in Christian giving. It indicates a great and serious need to teach the Word of God clearly and precisely in informational and educational stewardship forums and in personal confrontations. It reveals a need for bringing the Law and the Gospel to bear more strongly and more often.

God Comes First

The Word of God clearly shows that the material dimensions of human well-being are realized only when sound spiritual principles are adopted: "Seek first His kingdom and His righteousness [forgiveness of sins], and all these things [material benefits such as groceries, home, clothes, and car] shall be yours as well" (Matt. 6:33 RSV). Thus Jesus answers the question, "Who comes first?" He also gives the promise that God will take care of those who seek Him first. This is the great spiritual and radical *principle of living* which God has made part of life itself. It has God's promise that He will provide our real needs.

People tend to turn the two parts of Matthew 6:33 around as they seek first "the other things" (food, drink, clothes) and then as an afterthought hope that "the kingdom of God will be added unto them." The discerning Christian repudiates this basic error of man trying to sustain his own life by taking things into his own hands and ignoring God.

The most severe slavery, addiction, and sin we confront in life is addiction to mammon or possessions, the slavery to money, the sin of covetousness. More than any other factor in human life, the pursuit of money can corrupt the heart of man. It can dry up and shrivel a man's spirit, fill him with selfishness, make him cold and hard, drain him of love and compassion, and awaken in him jealously and hatred. Greed, covetousness, and avarice are always idolatry (Matt. 6:19-24), and, sad to say, many people are infected by it. Covetousness—the unrestrained desire to get what we do not have or what we cannot afford—harms and even chokes out our Christian faith. It closes our ears so that we do not hear the Word of God and apply it to ourselves.

While Jesus reminded us that "a man's life does not consist in the abundance of the things that he possesses" (Luke 12:15), the commercial world tries, to a high degree, to convince us of the opposite—that we cannot enjoy life unless we have an abundance of possessions. The Scriptures place adultery and covetousness on the same level (Eph. 5:3, 5) and tell us that neither one should be found among Christian believers, for adulterers and idolaters have no inheritance in the kingdom of Christ. Adultery and covetousness are diseases of the body and the spirit which eat away the faith of the one involved.

A pointed reminder for adopting priorities in our spending and placing God first is given us by Henry Drummond: "Above all else, do not touch Christianity unless you are willing to seek the kingdom of God first. I promise you a miserable existence if you seek it second." Many people are miserable even though they have growing incomes and both husband and wife may be working. They will continue to be miserable until God is placed first and they place implicit trust in His promises to feed and care for them.

The priority offering of a Christian is a repentant heart, for unrepentant sins and sinful habits hinder the stewardship life. Jesus tells us that if there is a sin of which we have not repented, we should first repent and seek forgiveness, and then offer up our gifts (Matt. 5:23-24). God tells us that the sacrifice He loves most of all is not the tithe or money offering from the hands of a sinner. First, God desires a broken and contrite heart and spirit—followed by our offerings (Ps. 51:16-17). Before we can run the stewardship race or continue in it, God tells us to throw off everything that hinders us, especially the sin that clings so easily and the sinful habit that holds us back (Heb. 12:1), which again points to the priority offering of a repentant heart.

The congregation of believers also needs to adopt priorities in the financial planning of the corporate church life: There needs to be a better coordination in spending for various projects, a turning away from self-interests to the most important priorities, stopping trends of fragmentation, and setting of priorities for the most necessary functioning and operating costs of the church locally and world-wide.

General principles that will help a congregation to set proper priorities in its expenditures: (1) what the congregation is committed to on the basis of God's Word; (2) the general commitments of the congregation in order to carry on a basic ministry to its own people and to the community; (3) care and discretion is to be taken in obtaining a proper balance in offerings for organizations and tasks to which the congregation is generally committed, but where no definite commitment is required to make a standard response.

Trust God—Believe!

All along the line there will be "practical" people who will maintain that the situation is tough, that people have too many material demands, that the job "can't be done," or that "now is not the time." The men and women of faith listed in Hebrews 11 faced various circumstances, and the inspired record tells how faith was followed by victory. These people all trusted God and as a result won battles, overthrew kingdoms, ruled their people well, and received what God had promised them (Heb. 11).

We face our present circumstances in faith no matter how difficult: Make new and revolutionary plans! Take radical financial steps. . . . Increase the salaries. . . . Trust God. . . . Build the walls of a new educational unit. . . . Quicken the debt repayment schedule. . . . Trust God. . . . Double the goal for World Missions. . . . Make prayers big, superbig! . . . Don't worry because people who have homes to pay for think they cannot give generous firstfruits, but teach them God's Word. . . . Believe God will help members change attitudes and habits so that God comes first in their budget. . . . Do we realize that we "have not because we ask not"? Do we know, "Ask, and it shall be given you"? (Matt. 8:7) . . . "If you have faith like a grain of mustard seed, say . . . to yonder mountain, move, and it will be moved" (Matt. 17:20). God will never let our earthly situation make a liar out of Him. Just believe! The Lord Jesus said, "According to your faith be it unto you," not according to your income be it unto you.

3. System

There are three requisites for a successful system in stewardship: A personal commitment or pledge; aggressive pastoral and lay leadership; and a definable program.

Commitment

We learn about Christ's expectations of commitment in Matt. 21:28-31, where He tells about the response of two sons to the request to "work in the vineyard today." The first son apparently became angry at the request and said he would not go, but later he repented, changed his mind, and went. The second son told the father that he would go, but didn't do it. When Jesus asked which of the two did the will of the Father, His audience answered, "The first." Jesus then compared them with the second son, who talked big but failed to come through with the promised action and obedience. Jesus said that thieves and prostitutes would go into the kingdom of heaven before they did. This is a very serious indictment because there are many Christians who attend church regularly and join in the Creed and general commitment, but they do not obey or act. It is tragic that such people face such a severe condemnation.

Life presents a third son who says that he will go, and he goes. Church members should be challenged to be the third son by God's grace. If they choose to be like the first or second son, we should plead with them to be like the first. This means that they may get angry at the stewardship message or challenge it, but after reflecting that it is their Savior asking them to work in the vineyard today, they will repent, change their mind, and go to work.

It is vital that every Christian make a definite commitment as to the use of his income and offerings for God. A definite commitment in terms of a percentage of his income for God is vital in order that the new man might tie down the old man, who always seeks to destroy any and all good intentions.

Aggressive Pastoral and Lay Leadership

Leadership for successful programs means a partnership of pastor and lay leaders in acceptance of and accountability for performing required tasks. If either one fails to exert effective influence, it will be difficult to attain mobilization of the entire membership and success in the stewardship efforts.

A Definable Method

Successful congregations vary their methods and organization of their program, but whatever approach they use, they organize it well. They may use an every-member visit, or group discussion meetings, or another method, but in any case they plan well and execute their plan effectively so that all members are reached with the message.

Laymen as Christ's Servants

Laymen can go a thousand times where the pastors can go once. Laymen can do so much more than the clergy because there are so many more of them—possibly more than 150 to 1. We need to get back to a fresh acceptance and vision of the true ministry of all the people of God, and the true ministry of those called and set apart by the congregation for the office of the public ministry. A high doctrine of the laity demands a high doctrine of the clergy.

God uses all of His people—laymen and clergy alike—as His instruments to bring spiritual blessings to the world. The whole church shares Christ's ministry in the world, for all Christians are priests for the world (1 Peter 2:5, 9). Priests should function first of all in the personal life, then through the congregational life.

As for the pastor, he usually is so loaded with duties that a distinctly spiritual and doctrinal ministry is well-nigh impossible. In many cases he becomes a packhorse, struggling under organizational burdens. The pastor as chief shepherd is to guide and counsel people in their tasks through a careful educational process. The pastor is to organize, deputize, and supervise, but not to do the work himself. He is called to teach and preach the Gospel, first of all.

The children of Israel often failed to respond or submit to God's dealings with them or to heed His prophets, as they rejected His ownership of them and His lordship. Jesus also actively portrayed the accountability to God as He portrayed God as the "owner of the vineyard" who "lent it out to cultivators." Jesus is the "chief agent of life" and "there is no salvation in anyone else." [4]

Someone has said that any Christian who is not actively involved in sharing Christ or serving Him has broken his contract of service with God; he is on strike against God. The body which does not function for its head is a sick body. Any parts of the body that do not function effectively

120

and are not coordinated with Christ, the Head, need to be restored and awakened. A Christian who is not an active steward in service to the Lord is like a cloud which brings no rain, a stove that gives no heat, a fountain that gives no water, a home that has no love.

Effective Stewardship

Some church members feel they are good stewards and managers when they give large sums of money, tithe, meet their individual pledges, meet the church budget, or build some facility. This evaluation is not valid. It is wrong to equate successful stewardship with specific programs or actions.

People usually think of stewardship as being a matter of *giving*, but it is really a matter of *taking*: We give nothing up but sin and selfishness. We take God's free grace and love, and we take the power and strength to give. That is the real secret of Christian stewardship.

Mother Superior in *Sound of Music* said: "Maria, you have a great capacity to love. See that you use this gift according to God's will." This love is not to be confined within the walls of the church, but free to move out into the world and into the life of every man. God has given all of us a certain capacity to love and to give.

Some money is used for our cars, houses, bowling, smoking, and various luxuries which should be placed on the offering plate. Joe is a typical church member, who in the past 20 years yearned $200,000. Twenty years ago he gave $50 a year to the Lord, and today he gives $200 a year. He has given a total of $2,500. If he had at least tithed, his giving would have amounted to $20,000. A deficit of $17,500 in 20 years!

Books and Materials as Resource

Readers who desire a full study of the grace concept of stewardship as outlined in this chapter may read *The*

Stewardship Call (Concordia) by the author. Program materials and booklets for every-member visits are available from the Louis Neibauer Company, Benson East, Township Line & Old York Road, Jenkintown, PA 19046: *The Big Step Forward, Let Love Guide You,* and *It Happens in Your Heart*. Booklets with vital stewardship messages are available for home visits or group meetings at the church.

Notes to Chapter 9

[1] 2 Cor. 8:1-14; Gal. 1:15-16; Eph. 4:7; 2 Tim. 2:1.

[2] Richard R. Caemmerer, *Preaching for the Church* (St. Louis: Concordia, 1959), p. 15.

[3] 2 Cor. 5:14; 8:9; 1 John 4:7, 10.

[4] 1 Sam. 8:7; Is. 33:22; Ezek. 20:13, 30-32; Luke 20:9-16; Acts 3: 15-18; 4:10-12; 5:30-32.

Chapter 10

The Gospel for Our Neighbors— Evangelism

Someone has said, "The real solution to any problem on earth is always a simple solution." When a Christian and a congregation establish evangelism as their greatest priority, they will have settled their basic problem. A confusion in establishing priorities is doubtless one of the bewildering problems confronting churches today.

No amount of programmed activities and official meetings of the church can take the place of day-by-day personal evangelism. Evangelism rightly conceived and properly practiced is as basic as Christianity itself. Every person must be active in evangelism because he is to be a disciple of Christ.

A Divine Imperative

The Gospel is a sacred trust from God. God requires of the Christian to be true to the Gospel, which is to be truly believed and proclaimed, and earnestly and effectively communicated. The concern for people and their needs flows from a proper appreciation of the role of the Gospel in the life of man. "Because of our love for you, we were ready to share with you, not only the Good News from God but even our own lives" (1 Thess. 2:8 TEV).

Gospel witness is the outcome of an inner spiritual power and of a genuine experience of Christ's salvation: "For we cannot but speak the things which we have seen and heard" (Acts 4:20). This witnessing is not a dogmatic discourse. It declares the things heard and experienced as personal realities through Christ. There is nothing as electrifying as a live, dynamic witness of what one has experienced through faith in Jesus.

While witnessing is a human art, it is, above all, a divine gift in and by the Holy Spirit. Every Christian can learn to witness, even though not all witnessing will be equally acceptable and effective. There are two basic requirements: some training and complete dependence on the Holy Spirit.

The New Testament makes it clear that salvation is an individual matter, a spiritual birth through a one-by-one process. Reaching all individuals in a community should be the all-embracing preoccupation of the church. Members should not think that their chief responsibility is to invite people to come to church. Their primary responsibility is to invite them to come to Christ.

Total evangelistic mobilization involves the 20-20 vision of Paul: "I kept back nothing that was profitable unto you, but have showed you, and taught you publicly, and from *house to house,* testifying both to the Jews, and also to the Greeks, repentance towards God and faith toward our Lord Jesus Christ" (Acts 20:20-21). This is the pattern for evangelizing the community and the world.

Evangelistic Emphases

Our aim is to live consistently, seven days a week, employing every available means to show Christ in our personal, family, social, and business lives. We are to engage in personal and public witness as God gives opportunity. Certainly, worship and Bible study together are basic, but the priesthood of all believers points to a climax in Christian work and witness in the world every day. Gatherings for worship and meetings at the church are to prepare believers for that ministry. It is the laymen busy everywhere in the world, not just gathered in the church building, who must truly represent the church and Jesus Christ to people who do not know Him.

Principles and Ideals

George W. Peters wrote in "Contemporary Practices of Evangelism" (an Issue Strategy paper for the International Congress on World Evangelization at Lausanne in 1974) about the abiding principles and ideals in evangelism: "The Gospel must be orally communicated, the Gospel must be demonstrated in life and action, and the Gospel appeal must be made personal. It must be made intelligible, meaningful, attractive, persuasive, and inviting. Gospel communication must be directed toward a verdict. . . . Every New Testament evangelism endeavor ought to face at least four basic issues: 1. Has the evangelism effort and endeavor brought renewal, revitalization, a new pulsation of the Holy Spirit to the local church communities? 2. Has the evangelism effort added new converts to the local church? 3. Has the evangelism effort eventuated in a movement or has it remained one great event in the community? 4. Has the evangelism effort facilitated the continued ministry of the local churches in the community? . . . Ideal New Testament evangelism, while flexible and adaptable, is undergirded by a firm structure which rests upon definite principles: mechanics, dynamics, bridges, operation, evaluation. . . ."

Michael Green in his Lausanne Congress Biblical Foundation paper, "Methods and Strategy of the Evangelism of the Early Church," wrote about methods in the New Testament church: "1. They worked from the center outwards. . . . The policy of so much modern evangelism is to drag people from the outside inwards; their policy was the opposite—to move from the inside outwards, and to evangelize, not on their own ground, but on other people's. 2. They were involved, yet mobile. It is fascinating to find that in the early centuries of the church there was no division between those who told the Good News and those who only listened to it. All were involved in the mission. . . . 3. They used their influence. . . . 4. They exercised oversight. The apostles supervised their converts, they set up presbyters to look after them, they wrote letters to them, they sent messengers to them, and they prayed for them. . . . 5. They produced witnesses." At the Congress, Green stated: "There is only one strategy in the New Testament: Obey the voice and Spirit of God!"

The evangelism program should include recruitment of special callers, intensive training, being energized by the Holy Spirit. Every Christian should be given a plan how to approach non-Christians, for this gives him the advantage of knowing what reactions and responses to expect from the prospects. It helps guide the conversation and allows the Christian to stay on the target and work systematically toward presentation of the way of salvation. It leaves the Christian free to analyze the prospect's answers and responses, and measure his understanding. Thus the witness is not desperately wondering what to say next and he is not in a quandary when he asks himself, "How will I bring up the matter of Christ and the way of salvation?" Also, a memorized approach step-by-step makes it simpler for him to say what must be said. It will tend to make fear disappear.

Rather than opening a conversation with someone abruptly and pressuring him with surprise questions, such as, "Are you saved?" the Gospel-bearer should begin in a low-key manner. He will meet the non-Christian where he is theologically, not where he desires him to be. We will never begin at the point of maximum conflict, but at the point of greatest interest. His procedure then continues with questions which lead to points of misunderstanding regarding the way of salvation and closes with a warm invitation to accept God's way of saving one and all.

Mobilize All Members

Evangelism requires the mobilization of all believers in Christ's church. Kenneth Strachan proposed a theorem which should be accepted and practiced by all churches: "The success and expansion of any movement is in direct proportion to its success in mobilizing its total membership and constant propagation of its beliefs." The plan is to utilize the total resources (all members, plus money and materials) of the total church in the task of evangelism. The four key words are mobilizing, constant, propagation, and beliefs. If beliefs are worth anything, they cannot be hidden or forgotten. They must be appreciated enough to propagate them. If beliefs are worthy, unique, and a matter of life and death, they must be shared constantly.

The theorem on mobilization of all members for evangelism should be printed and repeated in pieces of literature and on posters so that every member is fully aware of the necessity and intensity of the congregation's evangelism approach. All members are involved, and they should know it.

Mobilization does not mean that only a few leaders or activists are to be busy evangelizing, but that a plan is devised whereby all members communicate their Christian faith daily. Such a plan of mobilization indicates obedience to the Great Commission to go out to the whole world and proclaim the Gospel to every creature. It demands intensified and coordinated efforts so that a congregation's area of responsibility will feel the impact of its efforts. Every single person in that area should come to know that Christians are concerned about speaking of and for Christ.[1]

Let the community hear Christ's name and His Gospel incessantly. This will be done first of all by personal witness, radio, TV, films, dramas, Bible distribution, public lectures on the Christian faith, special missions for university students, rallies for young people, summer schools and Saturday schools for children, open-air preaching, and mission-emphasis weeks.

There should be a hard core of people in the congregation who witness about Christ. Also, the entire staff should spend some time each week witnessing formally and informally. Sunday school teachers should do the same. Billy Graham once told a group of ministers: "If I were a pastor of a congregation, I would pick out 12 men and train them, be with them, share my burden for souls and my feelings with them, until I have multiplied myself 12-fold. That is a Biblical pattern. It is what Christ did."

One pastor decided to put the idea into practice. He first selected three members and arranged a breakfast meeting with them at a restaurant close to their work. Each week another man was added to their number, to whom the pastor would present basic material and ask for a commitment "to become a partner in personal witnessing." A man is asked to make a threefold promise: 1. To witness to men of Christ; 2. To list names of those to whom witness is given; 3. To pray daily for the people on this list. "Hearing firsthand the experiences of others is a constant reminder that the Lord by His Word and through our witness and prayer does change lives," said one of the men. The men tell of their frustrations and their victories. They discuss ways of dealing with different situations, how to turn a congregation in a progressive direction, what Bible verses to use in various cases, and how to approach a person naturally.

Campus Crusade for Christ adopts Strachan's theorem of mobilization of all members and constant propagation of the Christian faith. Bill Bright, founder and president, writing how this organization is unique and "radical" told us: "In our objectives and goals it is our desire to be a catalyst to the Christians of the world in a commitment to help fulfill the Great Commission. It is necessary that we mobilize Christians and churches around the world." Bright added that some of the unique objectives are:

"1. The stress on the fulfillment of the Great Commission in this generation, with a target date of 1980.

"2. The emphasis on systematic strategies, planning, and evaluation to accomplish the task.

"3. The practice of aggressive evangelism and follow-up.

"4. The stress on the ministry of the Holy Spirit appropriated by faith in the life of the believer.

"5. The principle of multiplication through committed disciples who build and send others.

"6. The stress on training people in the 'how-to's' of Christian living and ministry.

"7. Our commitment to principles of national leadership in the various countries where we work (many mission boards have talked about this but very few are committed to its implementation).

"8. The commitment to the cultural relevance of our ministry and materials in various countries.

"9. A refusal to engage in 'negative criticisms.'"

Answering our question how he sees the nature of Christianity as "radical" compared to other religions and philosophies of the world, Bright wrote: "First of all, I see Christianity as different in that it is God's method. Most other religions and philosophies are committed to changing man's outward condition in the hope that man can be changed in the process. Christianity alone truly sees man as needing a radical change from within. And Christianity alone provides the means for such a change through regeneration and forgiveness. Christianity is concerned with the social needs of man but believes a permanent change can be effected only through a transformation of man's nature by the power of the Holy Spirit.

"Love is the need of the world, but true AGAPE (God's love) can only be achieved by Christ working in and through the believer. Christianity alone brings the liberation of man from bondage, and true freedom in the Spirit.

The followers of various other movements, such as Communism, and philosophies, such as 'yesterday's rationalism' or 'today's irrationalism,' are ultimately doomed to bondage. Even Christianity wrongly interpreted—such as legalism or antinomianism—can also lead to bondage. But if Christ 'shall make you free,' you shall be free indeed."

World Home Bible League

Ted Raedeke, formerly Key 73 director and now program director for Project Philip, wrote us about the evangelistic mission of the World Home Bible League:

"The World Home Bible League was founded by William Chapman in 1938. In the eyes of men Mr. Chapman was a successful realtor. In the eyes of God he was a dismal failure. God dealt with Chapman on a hospital bed. Standing at death's door, Bill vowed to embark upon a special ministry if God would restore him to health. His restoration to health gave birth to the World Home Bible League.

"On Good Friday in 1938, with a supply of 1,000 Bibles, Mr. and Mrs. Chapman went from house to house in Walkerton, Ind., asking, 'Do you have a Bible?' 'If we give you one, will you read it?' With this the Chapmans launched a Bible distribution ministry now totaling more than 10 million Bibles and Bible portions distributed *annually* by the World Home Bible League.

"The World Home Bible League is unique because it is not only concerned about the distribution of the Bible. It also has an equal passion that people are taught the Bible. John DeVries, a parish pastor with a zeal for evangelism, developed a method of inreach and outreach through Bible study and Scripture distribution called Project Philip. Its purpose is to teach the Bible with specially prepared Bible studies.

"Project Philip helps congregations to fulfill the Great Commission by 'teaching and reaching' with the Bible in 'Jerusalem'—those within the geographical area of the congregation. Project Philip also helps congregations to fulfill the Great Commission by 'teaching and reaching' people in 'Judea and Samaria,' through a motel and hospital ministry. Project Philip affords congregations the opportunity to carry out the Great Commission by 'teaching and reaching' people for Christ also in the far corners of the world, particularly through Project Philip in India. During the next 10 years the World Home Bible League has established a goal of 60 million dollars to provide 60 million Scripture packets consisting of a New Testament and four lessons written particularly for the unchurched. These will be provided in 14 major languages.

"Project Philip—a division of the World Home Bible League—got its name from Acts 8:30-31, where Philip asked, 'Do you understand what you are reading,' and the Ethiopian said, 'How can I unless someone teaches me?' Project Philip is training people, then distributing the Bible and teaching it to non-Christians.

"Project Philip has been richly blessed by God in foreign lands. In Mexico 100 churches cooperating in Project Philip over a two-year period gained 11,200 new church members. In Angul, India, one woman last December personally instructed 600 people, and most of these accepted Christ as their sin-atoning Savior."

John DeVries, international director, wrote: "A group of women in a little village, Zeeland, Mich., decided to advertise the WHBL Bible course in the *Reader's Digest* in India, in the English language. For the past five years they have placed an ad in the December issue and now are corresponding with 55,000 students! God has opened the doors for a number of ordinary housewives in a predominately Christian community in the Western world to carry on a unique personal ministry with thousands of the elite class in India. *This entire ministry is done on a completely volunteer basis!*

"Following their example, other groups of women in

Caledonia, Mich., a little town near Zeeland, placed three ads in the *Reader's Digest* in the Philippines and now have a school of over 10,000 students.

"A small group of women in Wellsburg, Iowa, placed a paragraph offering the Bible course in an annual book called *1001 Things for Free.* During the first year they received over 1,000 requests and now are corresponding with students in every state of the United States and several foreign countries!

"Each month, through a unique motel ministry, tourists walk off with 100,000 New Testaments from motel rooms. They are encouraged to do this! 'Reach Out' New Testaments are placed in the motels by churches participating in the WHBL motel ministry. Each Testament has an insert in it urging the tourist to take the Scriptures home and enroll in a Bible course sent by the local church.

"Every summer hundreds of teens are involved in 'TIME'—*Teens in Meaningful Evangelism.* Many of them go on weeklong bike trips, canvassing cities which they pass through. One TIME teen established a new world's record for distance last summer, pedaling 192 miles in one day. The teams, numbering about 30 young people, enroll between 500 and 1,000 students during an average week.

"While the opera *Jesus Christ Superstar* was playing in New York City, 20 churches organized themselves to distribute a tract entitled, *'Jesus Christ Superstar*—You've Heard the Opera, Now Read the Book!' The tract invited people to write for a copy of the first book ever written about the life of Christ, now translated into modern English (the Gospel of Mark) along with a study guide. These churches now have students from all over the world due to this unique ministry."

Various groups have also used the Home Bible Study approach in presenting the Gospel to the unchurched. It is very simple as friends and neighbors are invited by a

Christian host and hostess to their home. Business associates should also be invited. Under the leader's guidance a simple exegetical or topical study is presented. Participation is encouraged and questions are answered through the Scriptures. The study is always directed to the fact that people need Jesus Christ, and how Christ can be received. After the study, discussion continues among individuals as they remain for refreshments. It is the principle of teaching in the home. Follow-up calls are made as possible and necessary.

Congregations and leaders will want to keep in mind the provocative statement made by Bob Pierce: "God deliver us from anything that does not result in winning them to Christ." Yet fewer than 5% of church members consistently witness and participate in the practice of evangelism. Small wonder that the average church has a pitiable record in winning people to Christ. The first-century church "scattered abroad and went everywhere, preaching the Word." The situation is so bad throughout Christendom that churches in general and congregations specifically would do well to declare an international and local emergency and embark on a "crash program" to mobilize all Christian personnel and resources now, train them, and send them forth. We face an advanced state of moral and social breakdown, and we cannot let secondary issues prevail in churches but must rather plan a strategic outreach on churchwide, nationwide, and international bases.

The Radical Happening at Coral Ridge

One of the fastest-growing congregations in the United States has been Coral Ridge Presbyterian Church of Ft. Lauderdale, Fla. Founded in 1959 by D. James Kennedy, the church grew out of apparent failure after it had dwindled to 17 members in its second year—when Kennedy accompanied an evangelist on home visits and gained experience in witnessing. Some years before, he was converted when he heard Donald Grey Barnhouse ask this question on a radio program: "Suppose you were to die tonight and stand before God, and He were to say to you, 'Why should I let you into My heaven?' what would you say?" Today that very question is employed in the "Evangelism Explosion" personal evangelism technique.

When Kennedy returned to Florida after his witnessing experience with the evangelist, he determined to put his discoveries into action. He conducted six weeks of intensive training to send the people out to gain converts, but instead they remained at home. Kennedy said: "Then God hit me on the head with the realization that I had three years of classes in the seminary but that it was only when I received on-the-job training in the living room that I learned how to do it." So he began to take laymen with him on visits, and it caught on. Thus a learn-by-doing approach was added to the intensive training, and even new converts are given four months of instruction and are told that they are, in the words of the late Dawson Trotman, "Born to reproduce."

Listening Teleministry for Christ

There are Christian telephone counseling services such as "Contact Teleministries USA," which now operate in 63 cities in America with over 6,000 telephone workers responding to thousands of callers daily. This is a Gospel mission which offers a ministry of presence, of listening, of comfort, of Good News. There are 40 such ministries in other countries, and they are named "Lifeline Centers." The author is on the board of one such Contact center for telephone ministry, "Dial Now," of Milwaukee.

The objective of this Christian witness and service grows out of the challenges facing the church to engage actively in meeting the various needs in society today. It gives opportunities for concerned Christians to direct their love and compassion for their neighbor in effective channels and provides another way to involve themselves in meaningful witness and service through evangelizing and answering man's basic need for restored relationship with God. It uses innovative ways of employing volunteers to close some of the glaring gaps in services to people in need, caused by the short supply of trained professional staff.

Referral to existing community and church agencies is an important part of the telephone counseling. Many agencies supply direct assistance for the specific needs of a caller. If an individual needs face-to-face counseling, internal counseling service is available. If any callers need support in addition to what they can receive from the agency called, a shepherding program is available for making regular personal contacts with the callers once a week up to a period of three months or more if necessary. Regular contacts by the shepherds enable the callers to face their problems or find a workable solution for them. Mostly, people are helped by the opportunity to speak to someone about their problems, and church members are benefited when they move out from and beyond institutional concerns. These members open their hearts through telephone counseling to those who are troubled, hurt, and distressed.

There are many problems which cannot easily be solved, but there is not a problem in the world that cannot be sympathetically listened to. The first priority of the teleministry is listening, then offering hope and peace through Jesus Christ. This is Good News for the lonely, the friendless, the despairing, also for those who call beset with the ordinary problems of life.

The Gospel teleministry approach is quite extraordinary in that it offers a radical approach to reach many people who will not seek the ministry of the church or of Christians in any other way than to reach for the phone, dial, and pour out their hearts to a loving person on the other end of the line. Millions more need such a radical ministry now.

Robert E. Larson Jr., executive director of Contact Teleministries USA, Inc., writes about this church-related telephone counseling, crisis intervention ministry: "This ministry is unique in that Contact Teleministries USA represents the only national effort to promote and set standards for the development of such services. Many have copied and secularized our efforts, but through Lifeline-Contact (and through a similar service in England known as the Samaritans) the church was the first to use the telephone in this way. People are called to befriend the friendless, to encourage the discouraged, to support the weak, to listen to another person without judging, and to do all of this anonymously in the name of Christ and not their own."

Relation of Evangelism to Social Ministry

Evangelism cannot ignore man as a whole or the whole of society. Evangelism leads to a concern for man's social conditions. It is a matter of "both . . . and."

Our love for God requires our love for others. Our faith and love are tested when others have needs, and our faith should be expressed in generous assistance to those in need. "What does the Lord require of you but to do justly, to love mercy, and to walk humbly with your God?" (Micah 6:8). The Christian is to help the whole man, but this help is given with the principle which Jesus proposed: "Thy faith hath made thee whole." Unacceptable is a social ministry which does not present the Gospel and saving faith to make unwhole man whole. Only faith will make him whole. This truth places the ministry of the Word as the topmost priority. The church is to be known not chiefly for its community development activity, but rather for its ministry of the Word.[2]

Christians should not overlook the fact that injustices and human problems and needs are merely symptoms of a dreadful disease that the Bible calls sin. Because of sin, the heart of man is "deceitful above all things and desperately wicked" (Jer. 17:9). Jesus emphasized the fact that evil deeds originate from an evil heart: "Out of the heart of men proceed evil thoughts, adulteries, fornications, murders, thefts, covetousness. . . . All these evil things come from within" (Mark 7:21-23). The Christian church has the only message that will penetrate beneath the surface and reach the heart of man, leading toward a cure in society that will affect attitudes, actions, and the culture of man. As we show a concern and a positive approach for alleviating the ills of society, we must make sure that our primary method for accomplishing this work is through the proclamation of Jesus Christ.

God places a great responsibility on each Christian to show love in helping overcome social problems. Every Christian through the structures of society and government should be active in helping to alleviate social problems. The fruit of the Christian faith will be to focus on issues of personal and interpersonal relationships and to challenge secularism with the spiritual truth of Christianity. The church should teach ethical principles in the light of God's Word for individual decision-making. Thus Christians demonstrate to the community and world the meaning of personal wholeness and of a Christian community in coming to the aid of the neighbor both physically and spiritually.

The failure of some Christians to realize their social responsibility cannot be justified. It is not true that in order to fulfill one's social responsibility it is necessary to make evangelism a lesser priority or to adopt a humanistic theology. Meeting one's social responsibility simply means to carry out his Christian faith to its ultimate conclusions in his daily life. Obedience to Christ should lead one to explore the multiple opportunities for service to people in need. Christians as citizens should be involved individually in local and national government to alleviate injustices of all kinds.

Bishop Sheen once said: "We Americans need to justify our wealth by sharing it; theirs (the poverty-stricken) is the burden of being underprivileged; ours is the burden of being overprivileged." They die from undereating, and we die from overeating. Thus our prosperity is only an instrument to be used, not a deity to be worshiped. If only bankers can appraise our worth, then we are very poor. We should be appraised on the basis of active love and concern for our fellowman.

Christians have the responsibility to help safeguard the human rights of all people, to support all lawful authority, and to be informed about crime, delinquency, injustice, poverty, and other social problems in order to take active measures to correct them. The Christian faith is to be implemented socially, culturally, and politically.

Concern by all members should be evident by visiting the sick, feeding the hungry, clothing the naked, and helping the underprivileged. Concern is to be shown for those who are imprisoned by many of the disasters of life, such as poverty, discouragement, and the torments of the oppressed. Much heartache is experienced by millions, which should touch the hearts of Christians everywhere.

The inequities resulting in poverty and injustice spring from sin. L. Nelson Bell follows the example of Christ when he indicates from his own experience that it will do man no good after he is liberated from the oppression of illness and human structures if he remains internally and spiritually the same unregenerate man. Bell wrote: "For 25 years I shared in the work of a large mission hospital in China. During those years several hundred thousand patients went through the clinic and hospital. A great many of them had their diseases cured. Where are these people today—after a quarter of a century? Probably most of them are now dead.

"During the time these people were under medical care, the hospital staff carried on a carefully worked out plan of evangelistic effort. There was a prayerful and careful determination to lead these patients to Christ through word of mouth, the printed page, and example. Many of them accepted Him as Saviour and Lord either while hospital patients or later.

"Suppose all efforts had been centered on physically rehabilitating these patients without also preaching to them Christ as their Savior and their hope of eternity? Had this been the case, I would have to look back today on 25 years of futility, as far as eternal verities are concerned. . . .

"Emphasis on the temporal is a grave temptation, for it is this which we see and experience. Furthermore, if our Christianity is valid we must show forth love and compassion in ways that really help men in their social and physical misery. . . .

"Hungry men, thirsty men, needy men constantly enter the doors of a church only to hear economic, political, and social platitudes and panaceas. They are not fed with the bread of life, nor have they been able to drink from the fountain of living water.

"Our Lord says: 'This is life eternal, that they might know Thee the only true God, and Jesus Christ, whom Thou hast sent' (John 17:3). Shall those who need God's greatest gift be offered nothing more than that which perishes with time? It's being done." [3]

Excerpts from a 9-page letter signed by eight officers of the Evangelical Mekane Yesus Church of Ethiopia addressed to related donor agencies through the Lutheran World Federation stress the same: "It has become evident over the last few years that the churches and agencies in the West are prepared to assist in material development, but have little interest in helping the church meet her primary obligation to proclaim the Gospel. . . . A one-sided material development is not only self-deceiving in the sense that man needs more than that; it is also a threat to the very values which make life meaningful, if carried out with no intention to simultaneously meet spiritual needs. . . . Man's primary need is to be set free from his own self-centered greed. Here is where the Gospel of the Lord Jesus Christ comes in as the liberating power. . . .

"The Mekane Yesus Church in Ethiopia feels the time has come to call the attention of the Lutheran World Federation to this issue. It is our firm conviction that assistance should be brought into balance. . . . The division between proclamation and development which has been imposed on us is, in our view, harmful to the church and will result in a distorted Christianity. . . . We want to proclaim Christ because we believe it is our responsibility . . . because our people are hungering for Him."

Jesus does not only heal our sin-soiled souls, but He also heals troubled minds, sick bodies, and broken relationships. Christ, the Great Mediator, not only brings us to a restored relationship with God, but He also uses us to bring the Gospel of reconciliation to others so that they can enjoy wholesome relationships in life. Therefore Christians are involved in the healing process of restoring the broken harmony in body, mind, and spirit for proper functioning in the world and with God.

Christians and churches will want to undertake a healing and social ministry that makes an impact on the great need of our day. "World Vision" provides an excellent example to churches for conducting such a ministry of their own. We asked W. Stanley Mooneyham to tell us about the "essential nature and uniqueness of World Vision." He wrote:

"World Vision International is an international Christian humanitarian service agency committed to meeting human physical and spiritual need in the name of Christ. In a world of all kinds of overwhelming problems, we know

141

that we cannot do everything. But we also know that we can do *something*, and we feel that if we reach out to humanity, sincere in the belief that to help one person is truly significant, then our reaching will truly help many.

"Our philosophy can be summed up in two words: leadership and service. World Vision seeks to be a catalyst and an enabler within the church, helping others to help themselves and stimulating them to a broader vision of the world, its needs, and their own capabilities and responsibilities in meeting those needs. In doing this, World Vision seeks to demonstrate leadership, to show by example what can and should be done in Christ's service. As a servant of the church, World Vision works with and through others, not competing but helping, being a channel through which Christians may share their resources with those who have so little.

"In our activities we seek to be cooperative, flexible, noninstitutional, and indigenously oriented. We desire to cooperate with other agencies and to work through and with them whenever possible. As a result, we are able to have relationships with Christian agencies across the theological spectrum, as well as with private and governmental organizations, while maintaining our theological position of historic evangelicalism. We strive for a flexibility that will allow us to respond quickly and effectively to needs. We are not "locked in" to any system, ministry or method and therefore are open to attempt whatever is required to help and enhance.

"We recognize the need for, and value of, institutions but we generally seek to support them through and with other agencies. This non-institutionalizing of our involvements further contributes to our flexibility. Our commitment to an indigenous orientation means that we keep Western involvement and profile to a minimum, accept local cultures, use local Christians in responsible positions, and desire programs that are capable of local control and support.

"We believe that World Vision, as a Christian service organization, is unique in several respects. From our beginning, we have sought for balance and integration between the proclamation of the Good News of salvation in Jesus Christ and the concern for physical needs, the offering of "a cup of cold water" in Jesus' name. The Gospel contains two mandates: witness and service. We believe that to be true to the concept of the whole gospel for the whole person, both must be carried out. At the same time, our aid is not contingent on an overt opportunity to present the Gospel. We give assistance because people are in need, and not as a "lever" to present the Gospel to them. Yet God often makes that possible anyway.

"Among the almost 600 North American Protestant agencies with overseas ministries, World Vision is the largest service agency in terms of dollar income. This large dollar flow is accompanied by a diversity of programs that is probably unparalleled, ranging from child care to higher education to management training to crusade evangelism to disaster relief. There are major programs in 25 nations, with emphases in child care, emergency relief, community development, Christian leadership training, evangelism, education, information, and motivation (these last two directed largely to Christians in supporting countries). In making one-time grants, World Vision has probably contributed to every known type of Christian ministry. For the size and complexity of its ministries, we have a surprisingly small expatriate staff. Of the approximately 250 persons serving in five supporting nations, about 20 serve in management positions as expatriates in other nations. There are over 3,000 non-Western persons supported by World Vision who work within their own countries, about 600 of these in supervisory and management positions.

"We strongly believe that the local church can and should be better informed and able to become involved with meeting world needs. Through seminars, films, publications, and speakers, World Vision tries to show local churches how they can pray and think and respond more effectively and intelligently, both through their own channels and through agencies such as World Vision. We believe that this response need not detract from the church's own efforts. For example, the contributions to one church-based World Vision program are shared 60/40, with 60 percent going through the church to meet human needs and the remainder to World Vision programs. In short, we are willing to trust the Holy Spirit to be at work in their lives and willing to help them achieve what they believe He wants done in their individual and corporate lives.

"Catalyst—enabler—servant—channel; all terms to describe a truly international agency which allows Christians of several nations to become involved, in the name of Christ, with meeting the needs of a hurting world. All in all, our reason for service is not unique—but we believe our service is."

Evangelism should be supplemented by efforts to let a healing, feeding, self-giving Savior work through a great army of followers who give expression to His love in every situation.

The Christian ministry of the laity may take many shapes and forms as it penetrates the social structures through its members: industrial missions, penetration into the workers' "worlds" in the factories, high-rise apartments, offices, hospitals, dramatic and musical arts, and universities; meeting people in crisis situations, such as alcoholics, narcotics addicts, juvenile delinquents, migrant workers, refugees, and deserted old people.

144

Notes to Chapter 10

[1] 1 Thess. 2:4, 7, 11.

[2] James 2:15-17; 1 John 4:20-21.

[3] L. Nelson Bell, "Recurring Thirst," *Christianity Today*, XVII, 2 (Oct. 27, 1972), 36 – 37.

Chapter 11

The Gospel for the World—
World Missions

The Evangelization of the World in This Generation is even
more urgent today than it was in 1900 when John Mott
wrote his book by that title!

Many institutions and organizations provide greatly
needed services to people in their various needs. Only one
group or community, the church of the Lord Jesus Christ,
has the assignment to provide the message of salvation by
God's grace through faith in Jesus for all people. This is
God's plan. Man's tragic alienation from God and his
fellowmen is the reason for God's mission in giving Jesus
into death for humanity's salvation and in sending the
redeemed ones to share this Good News.

The world's population explosion presents a dramatic
opportunity for all Christians. From the time of the creation
of Adam and Eve until 1500 A. D., the population increased
to 500 million. From 1500 to 1830 (330 years) it reached one
billion. From 1830 to 1930 (100 years) one billion were
added for a total of two billion. Within 30 years—1930 to
1960—it reached its third billion. Within the last 15 years—
1960 to 1975—the world population has risen to 4 billion.

At every pulsebeat another human being is born into
the world. About one billion of the four billion claim to be
Christians (Catholics and Protestants combined). However,
most of the non-Christian population has never effectively
been confronted by the claims of Christ even once in their
lifetime. There are approximately 130 *nation states,* but
about 4,000 nations (*ta ethne*—tribe-language) and 2,000
languages which have no written alphabet and are without
the Bible.

146

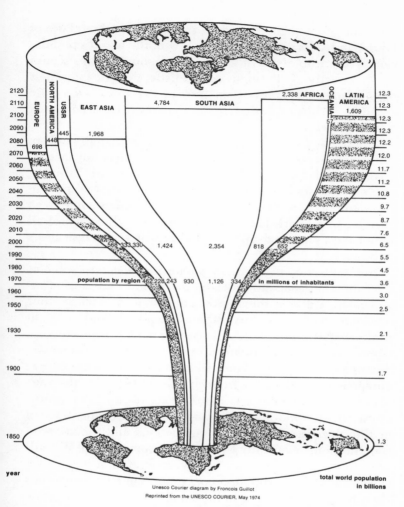

Unesco Courier diagram by François Guillot
Reprinted from the UNESCO COURIER, May 1974

THE CUP RUNNETH OVER?

This goblet-shaped diagram, prepared by the "Unesco Courier" on the basis of United Nations demographic projections, illustrates the growth of world population between the years 1960 and 2075 on a scale and with a speed unprecedented in human history. The almost exponential curve forms the bowl of the goblet. The width of the goblet represents the total world population. Note the sharp difference between population growth in the 1850-1960 period (stem of goblet) and the years following. A further constant growth period is apparent after the year 2075. The diagram shows eight major world areas along with their populations and indicates the year when the population in each will cease growing (around the year 2120 for Africa, with 2,338 million inhabitants; around 2070 for Europe, with 698 million inhabitants).

A tragic imbalance exists in the world, as about 90% of Christian leadership works with 10% of the world's population. We are told that if all Christian communities would reach effectively through evangelistic thrusts into their own communities, less than 20% of the world would be reached. Most non-Christians in the world have no Christian neighbors.

Many voices clamor to be heard — voices of nationalism, philosophies, political forces, religions, voices for materialism and pleasure. And people everywhere are listening and seeking for an authentic voice. They are real people who are born with a great spiritual need, people who hunger, play, hurt, laugh, cry, aspire, die. But most of all they have a gnawing spiritual hunger which is met in Jesus only.

We will do well seriously to consider together some of the following goals: to proclaim the Biblical basis of evangelism in a day of theological confusion; to examine our message and methods by Biblical standards and to relate Biblical truth to the crucial issues facing Christians everywhere; to strengthen our unity and love in Christ by diligent use of God's Word; to identify those who are yet unreached or alienated from the Gospel; to use the best patterns of evangelism as instruments of the Holy Spirit; to encourage churchwide prayer for world evangelization in this decade, asking all congregations and members to commit themselves fully to the Great Commission. We will seek to be a live church, a growing church, a witnessing church, a servant church, a concerned church, a generous church, a united church in mission.

Worldwide evangelizing and missioning is done through worship and church affairs, evangelists, reading rooms, radio and TV, ministry to universities, Bible women, literacy and linguistic work, printing presses, and transportation to mobilize the workers. The teaching mission is done through Christian schools, part-time agencies, Bible institutes, colleges, seminaries, conferences, retreats, adequate facilities, resources, materials, and equipment.

The ministry of love to those in need is carried out through hospitals, dispensaries, orphanages, world relief offerings of money and materials, Prince of Peace Corps with workers in agriculture, schools, etc.

Linguistic and Literacy Evangelism

Thousands are dying daily in tribal jungle ghettos, isolated from normal cultural and social relationship with their own countrymen and apart from those human benefits which the 20th century offers modern man. This is highly regrettable. But more tragic is the fact that these same people are dying without being able to read God's Word in their own language.

Science offers many marvels, but it cannot transform an illiterate, uncultured jungle tribesman into an integrated, functioning human being, socially fitted into the fabric of civilized society. Only a spiritual regeneration by the Spirit of God accomplishes that, by giving a person a totally new nature that makes him a new creature — a CHRIST-ian. The task of bringing such divine power to bear upon human impotence and satanic slavery is given to those who themselves have experienced this rebirth in Christ.

Reaching the untold millions still untold is truly one of the exciting and demanding assignments of our day, equaling the fascinating work of the great teams of men who have set out to conquer space. Most Christians do not seem to be aware that God has already deposited the natural and material resources into their lives for the thrilling mission task. As God brought Gutenberg and the printing press on the scene for the spread of Luther's translation of the Bible, so today He has supplied us with the gifts to translate and give His Word to every tribe throughout the world in our lifetime. These resources are: manpower, transportation, communication, and economic power. These resources were not given to turn America into a great playground for the natural man, but to be directed as instruments for a divine mission prepared especially for His called ones.

The Bible translation societies and their leaders stand as the Moses and Aaron of the modern age to call God's people to possess the land — to call God's people to their work and to develop the strategy by which the technical knowledge and ability may be employed to get the Gospel to the point of need everywhere.

Extraordinary is the open door of Gospel responsibility of performing a humanitarian service which various governments in underdeveloped countries find impossible to perform, even while they have erected barriers against regular mission work. The primitive conditions and the diversity of languages present a grave problem to governments unequipped to handle their responsibility to their own native tribes. Thus Bible translation has cultural, social, political, and economic significance beyond and apart from the spiritual task. Because certain governments accept linguistic and literacy teams for helping to integrate unreached tribes into their national life culturally and socially, a closed mission door is opened wide to bring a Christian message which is unwelcome under any other circumstances. Thus these governments become special instruments of God to employ evangelical Christians — the best ambassadors Christians can send — a true Prince of Peace Corps.

Christian history informs us regarding Jerome in a lonely translation room in Bethlehem, Wycliffe's monumental work in English, and Luther's poetic German translation in the Wartburg castle. The Bible today is no longer chained to tables in libraries for restricted study by scholars and students. It can now be placed into the hands of the most primitive native tribesman on earth. We have passed the pioneer days of a John Eliot with the Bible in the first

North American Indian tongue or a William Carey's first work in India's dialects. We now face a land to be possessed by faith by a people who hear the promise of their Lord, "In you shall all nations be blessed" (Gal. 3:8). The God who justifies the heathen through faith, even as in the days of Abraham, would have American Christians be a blessing to the unhappy, the fretful, the fearful, the guilt-ridden, the tension-filled lost ones—all who know not Christ.

The Rev. Eugene W. Bunkowske, linguistic consultant for the United Bible Societies in Nigeria, responding to a request to tell of the essence and unique nature and goals of linguistic missions, wrote: "At Christmas Jesus came for *all people*. On Good Friday He died for *all people*. On Easter He arose so that *all* might have the new life. On Pentecost God projected the incarnation across language and cultural boundaries. His Spirit jarred the apostles loose and made them linguists (language specialists who could cross language barriers with the great message). Immediately their witness exploded in the languages of people from all over the then-known world. Multitudes from many languages and cultures from Asia to Africa and to Europe accepted the NEW LIFE in Christ during those first dynamic years of witness.

"During the Middle Ages the linguistic approach to witness was shackled and the power and reality of God's purpose was locked away in the Hebrew, Greek, and Latin languages and cultures.

"Now in the last five centuries the witness is on the move again. During the past 50 years God has renewed the linguistic gift by giving His servants the ability systematically to learn, speak, write, and teach reading in languages that for centuries have been considered inferior and unworthy of God's special message. As dynamic oral witness, literacy and Bible translation move like a mighty tide from language to language, barriers of fear, hate, ignorance, and damnation are torn down. People of many tribes (cultures) and tongues (languages) are re-created in the image of Christ Jesus and rejoice with others across the world in becoming active witnesses.

"The goal of linguistic missions is to witness in such a way that the fulness of God in Christ will become incarnate (real and dynamic) for each person in the world without his being required to change languages or basic ways of life first. The approach of linguistic missions rests on the premise that God approaches man right where he is and when faith accepts God's gift of life all things become new and new ways of life and witness are the natural result.

"In the many cultures of the world which do not have the heavy bias against spiritual reality that Western culture has (African cultures, for instance), the process of receiving the joy and peace of salvation and the ever-increasing fruits of sanctification are wonderful to behold. In 1900 3% of Africa's population was Christian. In 1970 28% of Africa was Christian, and it is estimated that by the year 2000 46% of Africa will be Christian. Without linguistic missions this outpouring of blessings would not be possible. If this approach is used more consistently, it can be predicted that the harvest will be even more plentiful.

"The linguistic missionary is one who becomes incarnate in a language and culture which he did not possess from childhood. He uses the scientific tools of linguistics to understand the language and culture. He uses the vehicle of his acquired language to make the witness and lives in the culture effective in such a way as to give the people of that language and culture a MODEL of what the power, love, and forgiveness of God can do for anyone who accepts the Christ for whom he lives and of whom he speaks. Linguistic missionaries help new Christians grow in grace by encouraging oral witness, by analyzing the unwritten language, by preparing primers, Scripture materials and doing Bible translation as well as by encouraging the development of literacy programs, medical assistance, and other creative approaches to Christian living. Linguistic missions is a life committed to being a special messenger for God across language and cultural barriers to the very ends of the earth."

William E. Welmers, one of the outstanding linguists in the world—professor of linguistics and African languages at UCLA—commends the unique and radical contributions of the Wycliffe Bible Translators, Lutheran Bible Translators, the American Bible Society, and other groups. Welmers has made a unique contribution at the basic level of language analysis and language learning as a service to Christian missionaries and missions of churches.

Dr. Welmers told us: "Linguistics in the broadest sense is the study of the nature and structure of human language; human language is viewed as unique to and universal in the human race. Linguistics is thus also the study of the structure of individual human languages, which display some underlying universal characteristics, but also a vast array of diversity. In its application to the work of proclaiming the Gospel in the many languages of the world, linguistics involves first language analysis and language learning; it then addresses the problems of communicating the new concepts of the Christian message in languages in which those concepts have not previously been expressed, including the specific area of Bible translating.

"Linguistics in its applications in Christian missions is 'radical' in that it deals with that which is basic and essential to mission work: communication. The message which we communicate is, of course, basic and essential in another sense; but the message is useless if it does not reach the people for whom it is intended. Also involved is a radical departure from the popular assumption that missionaries can 'pick up' the languages of the people among whom they work, or that a native speaker of a language is qualified to teach it simply by virtue of his competence in using it. We recognize that learning a second language, as an adult, is quite different from learning one's first language in early childhood. The adult learner needs guidance in acquiring new speech habits and in recognizing and mastering new structural patterns that he was not prepared to expect. The skillful use of the tools of linguistics both speeds up and immeasurably improves the process of language acquisition and competence in the effective use of a new language in mission efforts.

"The Bible teaches that man is created in the image of God, and is thus a unique species. The unique and Godlike nature of man reveals itself in a number of ways; among those most commonly mentioned are man's moral sense or conscience, the nature of man's intellect, and the universality of religion in the human race. Less commonly mentioned, but I believe one of the essential aspects of the divine image in man, is language. Linguists and anthropologists, even if not Christian, recognize that language is species-universal and species-unique in man. Non-Christians have no explanation for this. One scholar helplessly attributes the origin of human language to some remarkable and inexplicable evolution of the neurological system. Another, after reviewing the various theories that have been proposed to explain the origin of human language, and writing them all off as silly, admits that we have no explanation *unless one wants to resort to a theory of creation!* My answer is, why fight it? Man has language because he is created in God's image. Christianity is unique among the religions of the world in its trinitarianism. The three Persons of the single Godhead communicate among themselves, and that is why man communicates in the way he does. Human language is what it is because man is created in God's image.

"A second aspect of this has to do with the variety of human languages. Although contemporary linguists believe that there are elements of universality in language, it remains true that there are many different languages. The diversity of languages, according to the Bible, goes back to Babel. The popular idea, however, that therefore the diversity of languages reflects man's sinfulness, and that uniformity would be ideal, is not a correct representation of the Tower of Babel account. God had ordered man to disperse and fill up the earth; man refused to obey that order, and tried to establish a restricted community centered in a tower. God, in confusing the language of the people, forced obedience to His command. Diversity in language is thus God's work, not initially man's development. Since the first imposed diversity, languages have continued to change and to diverge from one another. I believe this to be a natural phenomenon, not a specific result of sin; I believe that, if man had obeyed God's command to disperse, human language would normally have displayed something like the present diversity. Now, only Christianity provides a rational explanation for this. The philosophies and other religions of the world have viewed only one construction of the universe as ultimate and ideal: either unity or diversity (e. g., Plato or Kant or Buddhism versus pragmatism). Christianity is unique in recognizing, as embodied first of all in the Trinity, the equal ultimacy of unity and diversity: one God existing in three coequal persons. This revealed truth is reflected also in the nature of human language as it exists in God's image-bearers; the principle of unity is found in language universals, while the principle of diversity is found in the variety of language and language structures. Thus human language reflects the very core of Christian theology, the equal ultimacy of unity and diversity in the Trinity. Human language reflects and proclaims the glory of God."

World missions will thrive in a church where the whole counsel of God is proclaimed to acquaint members with the eternal and worldwide purpose of God, when people receive adequate information about that work, when leadership shows genuine concern and a readiness to act in faith. Leaders should think and live in global terms. While the task is colossal, the local congregation needs only to be concerned about active and effective participation by all its members.

George Peters has attempted to isolate the spiritual factors and the dynamic factors that need to be present in a church that is committed to Gospel outreach and mission advance. The necessary spiritual factors are: engrafted in Christ, nurtured by God's Word, and empowered by the Holy Spirit. The dynamic factors are: victorious prayer, fervor of evangelism, relevant messages, attitudes of expectation, triumphant faith, membership involvement, dynamic fellowship, rich worship experience, and proper priorities (putting God first). How does your congregation rate according to this proposal for a dynamic or radical group?

If there are to be vital and dynamic churches which take the Gospel to the ends of the world in our lifetime, there need to be dynamic factors in their everyday life and work. God's people cannot stand in the safety zone of the church and throw lifelines out to drowning men in the middle of the world ocean. The world situation today is driving us back to do an analysis that should help us to put first things first. If churches see their responsibility extending only to the limits of their own membership or even merely to their own community, to that extent they deprive the world of the saving Gospel and harm their own lives. A congregation which is not deeply and earnestly involved in the worldwide proclamation of the Gospel does not understand the nature of salvation.

Someone has said: "The light that shines farthest shines brightest at home." Complacency in many churches is a spiritual disease that paralyzes the effort for world evangelism. Every task of the church makes sense and has a purpose only as it leads to acceptance of its world mission outreach. The church is not asked to decide whether it will carry on the world mission or not, but only what priorities it will establish and how it will carry on this mission.

Christianity is confronted with sweeping revolutionary movements: nationalism, racial tension, economic upheavals, famines, increasing population, materialism, resurging religions. In the face of these circumstances, its task is still one: to present the saving Gospel of Jesus Christ to men and women so that, enlightened by the Holy Spirit, they may acknowledge Christ as Savior and Lord. Yet revolutions sometimes turn out to become a blessing in disguise; that is, when they cause people to become less self-reliant and more open to the acceptance of the Gospel message. Cataclysmic upheavals and great problems in communities in the world help loosen the iron grip of the old religions on the masses and create unparalleled opportunities for world missions. Revolutionary times make people hungry to learn new things and try new ways, to accept new suggestions and experiments with new ideas. At such a time Christianity can be shown to be the unique and radical answer and solution to man's basic problems.

Church Growth

"It is God's will that the church grow . . . that His lost children are found," states Donald McGavran. The Church Growth concept and movement is both Biblical and necessary. A responsible church grew out of the Gospel witness on the day of Pentecost. By the Spirit's power a worshiping, witnessing, and growing body came into being. However, later the letter to the seven churches in Asia expressed concern about a noticeable slackening of effort and a failure to grow, so that the continued existence of the churches as "candlesticks" was threatened. Witness and growth is to be expected until the end of time, when all believers will gather round the throne for praise.[1]

Churches fail to grow when leaders become victims of a fatalistic attitude and defeatism. Also, they fail to grow when they become prisoners of their buildings and lose their mobility, confining their activities within the walls of the sanctuary. Another situation that hinders growth is a "Family Clan" mentality, reaching only one specific culture and social group. Other real hindrances: when churches carry on the work of God more on the natural level than the spiritual, when they are self-centered, when they remain in bondage to traditions and religious habits, and when a pastor-do-it-all attitude persists.

Mission outreach and church growth are thwarted and retarded by too much dependence on paid workers, by too little training and participation of lay people, by too little sensitivity to the authority and strategy of the Holy Spirit, by acceptance of small results long after the larger response should have been expected. The church is also hurt when goals are inarticulate, inadequate, immeasurable, or unattainable.

Church Growth follows the New Testament pattern of human witness communicating God's message effectively by the Holy Spirit, resulting in numerical reproduction and geographic expansion. Robert Coleman sees in the Biblical blueprint of a well-defined mission, well-planned method, and well-trained men "the master plan of evangelism."

The presupposition for the Church Growth movement is that abundant reaping requires abundant sowing and that when Christians join together, work together, and pool their resources for evangelism God multiplies the believers. The principles involve mobilization of every Christian for witness within the framework of the church by the local leadership with global objectives. The plan itself dictates that resources be matched with the needs through creative programming. This is simply an aligning with the dynamic factors for growth inherent within the church in response to the will of God and the prompting of the Holy Spirit.

C. Peter Wagner writes that "the indispensable condition for a growing church is that it must want to grow." [2]

The hinge that swings the door of church growth is implicit faith in God and complete dependence on the Holy Spirit. This will lead to the "geometric progression" of 2. times 2 equals 4, times 2 equals 8, times 2 equals 16, times 2 equals 32, etc., etc., etc.

True church growth will find:

1. Your church will discover the abundant theological and Biblical foundations upon which church growth rests.

2. Your church will analyze its situation by clearing away the "flaws," getting at the facts, and considering the dynamics by which the church grows.

3. Your church will discover and apply trusted re-producible principles of growth, set goals, and establish priorities.

4. Your church will see new possibilities for growth in your unique environment.

5. Your church will formulate bold, exciting, and attainable growth plans with participants to help formulate and put into action.

Your church will grow by God's grace because members will want it to grow in obedience to God's will and because you are using strategy and methodology in making disciples. Then nongrowth will be called nongrowth, and growth will be accepted as a gift of God.

Donald McGavran offered us the following essay on "The Unique and Radical Nature of the Church Growth Movement." He wrote: "The Church Growth way of regarding Christian mission has exerted a remarkable influence on the entire missionary enterprise. It has sharply challenged the deviations which large numbers of mission leaders have espoused. It has estimated correctly the tremendous swing to the Christian faith in Africa and other large sections of the world. It has provided a theory and methodology which employs the insights of the modern sciences of man, while remaining openly and firmly committed to Biblical Christianity."

Dr. McGavran offers the following "Ten Prominent Emphases in the Church Growth School of Thought":

"1. The Church Growth School of Thought is deeply theological.

"Church Growth is born in theology. It arises in a certain view of God and man, sin and salvation, brotherhood and justice, heaven and hell, revelation and inspiration. The tremendous labor involved in Christian mission, the selfless outpouring of prayer and life that others might enjoy the benefits of right relationships with God as revealed in His Word, would never be undertaken for human reasons. As one looks at the history of Christian missions, he sees how closely the fortunes of the apostolate have waxed and waned with the rise and fall of spiritual vitality and Biblical conviction in the sending churches and denominations.

"Only those who believe that God wants church growth continue to send their sons and daughters abroad. Only an unmistakable conviction that God wants His lost children found produces or long maintains Biblical mission.

"Church growth thinking is poles apart from the theological rationale of mission which the ecumenical movement has promulgated during the past 15 years and which found such clear expression in the Uppsala Document 'Renewal in Mission.' The distress we voiced in the May 1968 issue of the *Church Growth Bulletin*, which asked, 'Will Uppsala Betray the Two Billion?' rises out of the heart of the Church Growth School of Thought.

"The official Geneva line in missions in un-Biblical fashion makes man the center of all things. Doctor Beyerhaus maintains that it does not so much deify man as understand God in human terms. It proposes that horizontal reconciliation alone is the program of missions. Despite tipping the hat in the direction of reconciliation with God, the new line in missions devotes itself largely, indeed, to alliance with revolutionary movements in the fight for social justice and toward the unity of all mankind. Metaphysical elements of Bible and theology have been de-emphasized, averring that these are meaningless to modern man, to a world come of age. The result is an existential humanism within the framework of a revolutionary philosophy of history, thoroughly camouflaged with abundant prooftexts exegeted in an arbitrary manner.

"These and similar deviations are — to be sure — not held universally. In most missions and churches many Christians remain faithful to the plain sense of the Bible and to its unity and authority. Nevertheless, the official line in missions has become similar to what I have described. Evangelistic missionaries are not returned to the field. Theological seminaries are staffed by men who find the Uppsala line agreeable. Tremendous current opportunities for discipling are easily set aside. Open doors are not entered. Winnable multitudes are not won.

"Because of its theological base, the Church Growth School of Thought recognizes and rejects all attempts to depart from the plain meaning of the Scriptures that men are lost, that God wants them found, that the way of salvation is solely through belief in Jesus Christ and incorporation in His church.

"Most Christians are unaware of the magnitude of today's deviations and have a trusting confidence that the good men leading their denominations and missionary organizations cannot be wrong. They believe it desirable to have new policies and news ways of stating the truth. However, they find it difficult to imagine that the particular new ways being discussed involve the destruction of the Christian faith.

"2. The Church Growth School of Thought advocates proportion in missions.

"It holds that men have multitudinous needs of body,

mind, and soul to meet, which is thoroughly Christian. The church is properly engaged in relief of suffering, pushing back the dark pall of ignorance, and increasing productivity. But such activities must be carried out in proportion. *They must never be substituted for finding the lost.* Christians must never be guilty of turning from the Spirit to the flesh or of deceiving men by offering them transient betterment as eternal salvation.

"In regard to the battle raging today between advocates of evangelism and social service, we say that finding the lost and bringing them back to the Father's house is a chief and irreplaceable purpose of Christian mission. It is not the only purpose. Remember the two billion, shortly to be three billion, who are living and dying without any chance to become disciples of Christ, without any opportunity to sit down at the Communion table and partake of the Medicine of Immortality. How shall they hear without a preacher, and how shall they preach unless they be sent? We also plead with any so devoted to vertical reconciliation that they tolerate horrible injustices which they have the power to correct, 'Inasmuch as you do it to one of the least, you do it unto Me.'

"3. The Church Growth School of Thought seeks to see the actual situation in regard to both churches and missions.

"It advocates action in view of the true facts. It deplores the vast discrepancy between theory and practice. It seeks to bring performance into line with promise. Both liberals and conservatives, faced with many human needs, often limit themselves to resistant populations. They are always bound by previous patterns of action, cumbered by institutionalism in advance of the church, burdened with cultural overhangs, and committed to a non-Biblical individualism. Often they are deceived by their own promotional efforts ("Whatever our missions do is wonderful!"). They entertain small expectation of church growth and they spend most of their budget, time, and men for other things. Church

162

Growth men are resolved not to deceive themselves with appearances but to press through to the facts.

"We preach that most worthwhile human efforts draw heavily on exact quantitative analysis and that the church should do the same. The church consists of countable men and women, and there is nothing particularly spiritual or meritorious in not counting them. To be sure, no one was ever saved by accurate membership counting; and no one was ever cured by a thermometer. Yet the physician always puts it in the patient's mouth. Statistics do not cure, but they tell a great deal about the condition of the patient. They enable correct diagnosis. They help dispel the fog of good intentions, promotional inaccuracies, hoped-for outcomes, vast generalizations, and general ignorance which hides the real situation from leaders and workers of missions.

"4. The Church Growth School of Thought believes we live in a most responsive world.

"Searching for truth, no matter where it may lead us, we have been pressured by the weight of evidence into accepting the revolutionary idea that during these decades the world is much more receptive to the Gospel than it has been in 1,900 years. This idea is enhanced when mankind is viewed as a vast mosaic of ethnic, linguistic, and cultural units. In almost every land some pieces of the mosaic are receptive to the Gospel.

"After E. C. Smith graduated from Fuller Seminary's School of Missions and returned to Java, his Southern Baptist mission embarked on a deliberate policy of starting 'thousands of house and hamlet churches among receptive Muslims and Chinese.' An Indian graduate, now serving on the faculty of the Hindustan Bible Institute, decided that it was feasible to plant 100 new congregations in Madras. I have often said that in Africa by the year 2000 there would be 100 million Christians. Dr. David Barrett thought my estimate was far too conservative. He proceeded, on my request, to do the demographic calculation necessary, and his estimate was 357 million Christians in Africa by 2000 A. D. (May 1969 *Church Growth Bulletin*).

"5. Despite this widespread receptivity, enough discipling is not happening.

"Paucity of knowledge concerning people groups, receptive populations, arrested Christian movements, the effects of revivals, and a hundred other aspects 'keep the church mission organism working in the dark concerning its God-given task. All kinds of theories as to the desirability of methods (such as dialog with non-Christian religions, industrial evangelism, and accommodation to culture) are propounded without adequate knowledge as to the effect these have on bringing *ta ethne* to faith and obedience.

"Enough discipling is not happening—this is typical of Church Growth thinking. Traditional missions take offense at the word 'enough' and like to consider lack of discipling as inevitable in view of the hardness of men's hearts. Church Growth people recognize, of course, that some fields are so resistant that no church grows; but they also recognize that often appeal to the difficulty to the field simply masks the fact that the church concerned is not seeking lost sheep or is resolutely looking for them in ravines where they are not grazing. In Chile, for example, all the old line missions are getting very little growth in a country where several hundred thousand have become evangelical Christians in Pentecostal churches.

"Church Growth thinking insists that our goals for the next 30 years must not be set in view of the long, slow exploratory periods in Christian missions. Defeats of the past are not to be our guide in estimating the future. In view of the tremendous growth of the new religions of Japan and other lands, we must give up the concept, canonized in many quarters, that the great ethnic religions of the world will continue to reject the Gospel.

164

"6. Emphasis on Research on Church Growth.

"Convinced that hundreds of millions who have yet to believe are diverted from knowing Christ through a paucity of knowledge concerning discipling, the Church Growth School of Thought lays great emphasis on scientific research to ascertain the factors which affect reconciling men to God in the church of Jesus Christ. We believe that tremendous discoveries await us there. Where have denominations grown? Where have congregations multiplied? Where have they *not* grown? How much—or how little—have they grown? Above all, *why* have they grown?

"7. Publishing Church Growth Studies.

"Church Growth men believe that the hard facts about church growth once discovered should be published, taught to ministers and missionaries, read by serious-minded Christians, and used in all evangelistic labors whether in the local churches or in nations. A firm foundation of facts needs to be placed under the missionary enterprise.

"8. Using the Sciences to Further Discipling.

"The Church Growth School of Thought lays great emphasis on using the social sciences—anthropology, sociology, psychology—to aid churches and missions in bringing the nations to faith and obedience. We use them for *further discipling*.

"9. The Church Growth School of Thought lays great emphasis on classical evangelism.

"We believe every form of it should be greatly increased. Personal evangelism, good-deed evangelism, newspaper evangelism, radio evangelism, evangelism in depth, and saturation evangelism—all are good. Circumstances dictate which form should be used.

"Church Growth thinking holds that when God sends men into ripe fields, He wants sheaves brought to His barn. He wants members added to His church and new churches started. If evangelism is not delivering them, something is the matter. Looking at it from God's side, evangelism is not faithful enough. Looking at it from man's, it is not effective enough.

"10. Revamping Theological Education.

"Church Growth theory maintains that a seminary is not a place where men learn subjects. It is a place where men learn how to nurture *and multiply churches.*

"Clark Scanlon insists that theological professors should themselves be competent church planters, as well as historians, exegetes, and theologians. Seminaries should engage their students and faculties in multiplying churches. Ralph Winter tells of the values of theological education by extension. It will train the real leaders of the churches, the laymen who now carry on the work, and will give them systematic theological training."

World Literature Crusade

Jack McAlister, founder and president of World Literature Crusade, has also developed a unique and radical Gospel mission. This missionary agency is attempting the impossible in reaching every home on earth with the Gospel and Christian literature. Having reached one of four homes on earth, over three million people have written the World Literature Crusade overseas, indicating a decision for Christ.

World Literature Crusade is a systematic house-to-house distribution of the Gospel of Jesus Christ by the printed page now going forward in 66 countries—where more than a third of the world's people live. It enjoys the cooperation of Christian nationals of 415 organizations and denominations overseas for the volunteer phases of the distribution in each country. The WLC name never appears on the messages it provides, in order to avoid the image of Christianity being a Western religion.

McAlister wrote: "WLC is committed to share the Bread of Life with *every creature*—especially with those on the back roads. The printed page is the most far-reaching effective tool in today's evangelism. There are five major reasons for this. First, it is economical. Second, the number of people who can read increases by leaps and bounds every week. Third, there is a magnetic power in printed words; people believe what they read. Fourth, it is permanent inasmuch as it can be kept and read over again, while a sermon preached soon fades from memory. Fifth, it offers a wide and common opportunity for a majority of Christians to partake in evangelism; a boy of 10 or a woman of 70 can do this work of distribution. Our hope of getting the task completed lies in LITERATURE—the Word of God and the Gospel message printed in the language of the people."

Every Home Crusade is an evangelistic movement usually supervised and conducted by national Christian leaders. It challenges and mobilizes Christians everywhere to pray, and offers an opportunity to "attempt the impossible" for God.

Outreach Through Radio

God has given Christians a tremendous resource for Gospel outreach through the mass media. Dr. Eugene R. Bertermann, executive director of the Far East Broadcasting Company (formerly serving as director of *The Lutheran Hour* and executive director of *This Is the Life*), and president of the National Religious Broadcasters for almost two decades, tells us of the unique contribution of Gospel Radio Ministries:

"The use of the modern electronic medium of mass communication is, we believe, in the finest of Reformation tradition. Dr. Martin Luther and his fellow reformers took advantage of the printing press—recent invention in their time—for spreading the Gospel of the Lord Jesus Christ. A writer in *Christianity Today* (May 22, 1970) asserts: 'Luther and his allies might never have caught the attention and support of the masses, had they not been able to distribute voluminous amount of literature pleading their cause.' It is, therefore, not surprising that the airwaves of radio and television are utilized today!

"The first religious radio program broadcast in the United States was aired by radio station KDKA, in Pittsburgh, Pa., which began operating in 1920. The Moody Bible Institute of Chicago began its radio station in 1926. The Lutheran Church—Missouri Synod began radio station KFUO in 1927. By the 1930s programs such as *The Lutheran Hour,* the *Back to the Bible* broadcast, and the *Back to God Hour* were very popular. Radio quickly became an accepted vehicle for the proclamation of the Gospel.

"Television, however, did not fare quite as well. One writer declared: 'No aspect of the American culture fares as poorly on television as organized religion. The economics of the medium, the secular mood of the writers and producers, and the lack of evangelical zeal in the vocational dimension—these combine to effect an ecclesiastical blackout on our living room screens' (*Christianity Today,* Jan. 16, 1970, pp. 24-25). However, *This Is the Life* has set an excellent record of proclaiming Christ through drama on television now for a quarter of a century. It was not until the last several years that religious television programs generally have come into their own.

"We firmly believe that God permitted radio and television to be invented or discovered, not first and foremost to sell a commercial product, or to carry an entertainment or educational program, but as a vehicle for the proclamation of the Gospel of the Lord Jesus Christ.

"Evangelical Gospel broadcasters on radio and television are organized into the National Religious Broadcasters. The purposes and goals of the organization are set forth in this declaration taken from its Constitution:

Recognizing the vital and increasingly important role played by radio and television broadcasting as an agency of mass communication, vastly expanding the potential audiences of the church and the classroom, the National Religious Broadcasters believe that the propagation of the Gospel by radio and television is essential to the religious inspiration, guidance, and education of the public, to the enrichment of the national life, and to the full use of this blessing of modern civilization in the public interest. In furtherance of this belief and of its purpose to foster and encourage the broadcasting of religious programs, and to establish and maintain high standards with respect to content, method of presentation, speakers' qualifications, and ethical practices, to the end that such programs may be constantly developed and improved and that their public interest and usefulness may be enhanced, the organization has adopted, and each of its members has subscribed to, a code of ethics.

"Gospel broadcasting today represents a broad spectrum of outreach by means of radio and television. Program producers in the United States and Canada, Great Britain, and Australia furnish Gospel presentations in many different formats. Domestic radio and television station owners and operators have developed attractive and compelling program schedules. And international Gospel broadcasters such as HCJB, Quito, Ecuador; Trans World Radio, Monte Carlo, Monaco; Bonaire, Netherlands Antilles; and the Far East Broadcasting Company, with 25 stations located principally in the Orient, transmit the Gospel in many languages."

General Considerations

Criteria by which people may make a decision as to whether or not to support a mission organization or the extent to which it is to be supported are to include the following: How doctrinally sound and evangelical is the organization? How is it being used to bring the saving Gospel of Jesus Christ effectively to non-Christians? Is it carrying on ministries which are not being accomplished by other organizations and is it not in competition with other organizations according to the overall need? Does it have a functioning board responsible for preserving its Christian testimony according to Biblical standards and is the operation of business policies sound?

There is a very important place for medical missions in the mission plan. Throughout His ministry Jesus repeatedly healed people: "And He healed him." Jesus made the blind to see, the lame to jump for joy, and the deaf to hear. The Great Physician also encouraged the disciples to heal. As a result, healing was often a part of the ministry in the early church and grew out of the preaching and teaching of the Word.[3]

Throughout the history of mission activity, healing and medicine have been connected with the work of preaching the Gospel. Medical ministries have sufficient reason for their existence because of their necessity. Moreover, our experience of Christ's love makes it even more imperative for us to be involved.

The question about a moratorium on sending missionaries must be answered with a resounding statement that the day of the missionary is not past. The Scriptures make it plain that missionaries are part of God's plan as long as there are non-Christians. The foreign missionary is needed and has a place on most mission fields now. Wherever the national church is not capable of taking over the total task of evangelization in its country, there is a place for the missionary. The national Christians will be benefited by the partnership of missions in reaching unreached areas. This is so vital because 83% of the people in the world do not have a next-door neighbor who is Christian. Most people are dependent on a missionary sent to them if they are to hear the Word of God.

Some people feel strongly about the fact that there are closed doors to missions, and sometimes it appears so. However, we cannot find much about closed doors in the New Testament. Possibly some people would say that there were closed doors under the Roman Empire when Christianity was attacked so vigorously and considered illegal. However, this situation turned out to be an open door to the Gospel. If there is a closed door, it is closed only so that it can be opened miraculously. As God's people pray and trust God, doors will be opened. It really is not the iron curtain or bamboo curtain that is stopping the church from missions, but very possibly it is the plush curtain of easygoing, self-centered materialistic living on the part of many Christians.

There is an apparent immediate need in the world for an intensified evangelization thrust that involves greater personal consecration and more sacrificial offerings from God's people. God has led us to a time in the history of man when we see the riches of His grace on the one hand and the spiritual poverty of the unnumbered masses on the other. Obviously, God claims more from His people than they have given.

Congregations should be challenged to set high mission goals—faith goals—to support world missions to send out more workers. There are basic questions that leaders should ask themselves and the group that sets the world mission financial budget before they make a final determination on what their goal shall be. We ask:

1. Have we prepared ourselves spiritually to cope with the responsibilities and opportunities that God has given?

2. How are we making it clear through our church programs that we are the pilgrim people of God commissioned to evangelize the world?

3. Did we spend adequate time to inform all members of the full mission opportunities in the world?

4. Have we had an effective educational program in proportionate giving and tithing to undergird world mission support?

5. Is our mission goal being set on the basis of a year-round mission education program, using all of the educational resources available?

6. Do we realize what our congregation's goal means in terms of what this will allow our church body to do for world missions?

7. Is our goal large enough to cause us to realize it will need more than budget appeals to meet the goal? Is the goal sufficiently challenging and the increase great enough to show that we can honestly pray the Holy Spirit to perform great things through us?

8. Is this a "faith goal" that will require nothing less than week-after-week prayer support in our church and day-by-day prayer support in our homes?

9. Does this goal test us to give the most effective leadership and does it challenge the best that is in us by God's grace?

Notes to Chapter 11

[1] Acts 2; Rev. 2:5; 7:9-17.

[2] C. Peter Wagner, "What Makes Churches Grow?" *Eternity* (June 1974), 17.

[3] Matt. 9:35; 10:1, 8; 15:3; Mark 1:25-34; Luke 17:15; Acts 3:11; 4:13-14; 9:34; 28:8.

Chapter 12

Human Intervention Distorts the Plan of God: Humanism and Naturalism Versus the Supernatural

We have discussed the great plan which God has designed for man's life in the world and for all eternity. But human nature, which has not and will not accept God's will, rebels against God's plan. Man proposes explanations of human origins and relationships that ignore or reject the divine and supernatural, thereby circumventing or destroying the mission of God by devising a humanistic plan.

The beautiful Divine Plan considered in these pages is sidetracked even by some churchmen, who are offended by the radical Biblical emphases which provide supernatural dimensions to life. Unless the Christian is aware of these tendencies toward naturalism in some churches, he may become an easy prey to mission distortions proposed by contemporary humanists and theologians. This study of the radical nature of Christianity would end up incomplete if the writer failed to point out how these tendencies dilute now and ultimately destroy Christianity and the radical mission of God.

Christians and Christianity exist in a world which presents many challenges and conflicts. Man's achievements in science and his philosophical ideas are sometimes so interpreted that they come into conflict with the Christian faith. Many options are available to be considered by the intellect, as secularistic and humanistic forces often contrive to make Christianity appear as hardly a viable option, if not as an absurdity. Sad to say, sometimes the humanists, secularists, and materialists are joined by acclaimed thinkers identifying themselves as progressive Christians who attempt to syncretize earth's value systems with Christianity as another viable option. They attempt to provide more "reasonable" and "acceptable" answers in order to avoid offending the pagan world and its cultures. It has resulted in attempts to offer a "new theology," that is, a syncretistic form of Christianity, a "culture Christianity" which has deleted some of the supernatural and radical Biblical essentials offensive to the unconverted human mind.

Knowledge and the thought process are gifts from God and are to be used as such in the decision-making process. Yet there are a goodly number of entities in life that are beyond man's comprehension and reason. It is imperative, therefore, that everyone must operate within the realm of faith as he accepts or rejects what he has come to know. The *Christian* religion is a faith religion. "It is by faith that we understand that the universe was created by God's Word, so that what can be seen was made out of what cannot be seen" (Heb. 11:3 TEV).

The Naturalistic World of Humanism

Humanism, both old and new, has been active in the thought world to challenge the supernatural and radical elements of the Christian faith. Some will often turn solely to science for mastery of their world, some to liberal education for mastery of their minds, others to diplomacy for mastery of their international problems, yet others to law for mastery of their criminal disorders, or to government for mastery of their economic injustices, or to revolutions for mastery of their racial tensions, or to something else. Moved by their naturalism, they will turn to themselves in order to save humanity rather than turn to God.

Humanism, ever since Aristotle, holds that when men have the proper information about themselves and their problems, they will try to make corrections. Christianity holds that men must be confronted with their sinful nature and realize that they are incapable of helping themselves and must therefore turn to Christ for a solution to the problems now and for the life beyond. Humanism appeals to the self-centeredness in man. Hence, its "gospel" concentrates on the reconciliation of man to man, for "sin" is considered man's maladjustment to man. Humanism approaches the questions of life on the horizontal (man's) level. All the grandeur and the facts of life's existence he has learned are for the humanist the sum total of human life.

Humanism is the appreciation of man and of the values of human life. Classic humanism, however, keeps God out of the picture altogether. So does the "new humanism," which views man as the ultimate reality and tries to come to expression by adopting theological formulas. These formulas are articulations of man's understanding of his own existence (anthropology), not affirmations about God. It tries to emancipate man from the dominion and authority of the supernatural and the Holy Scriptures, which prescribe obedience or set bounds to man.

The humanist may deny that he is an atheist or agnostic. Yet he simply leaves God out of the picture. He turns to other sources to understand his own origins and purpose. Man is no longer considered something set apart by God, but only a species of animal. In the light of God's truth humanism has succeeded in some ways to dehumanize man. From this situation stem many of our present problems. In contrast to false humanism, Christianity stands out and above as the religion that spells out man's rightful place in the universe.

The Synthetic World of the New Humanism

The "new humanism" emphasizes the possibilities man has of himself. It insists that many of the seemingly fixed patterns of human nature are actually cultural characteristics that can be changed, and it lives with highly provisional solutions. This humanism proposes the false hope that reason will tame and direct conflicts in life to produce positive results. When reason fails, science and pills are expected to do the job. Present-day humanism always wants to give reason another chance, for it has a passion that the secular is superior to the divine. Instead of saying that man should be filled with Christ and the Holy Spirit, it exhorts him to "be human."

The new humanism is the result of spiritual blindness. At its heart is the notion that anthropology (the study of man) can replace theology (the study of God). The humanist holds that he truly sees the problems of man and his world, and undertakes to solve them by natural means. He is preoccupied with the plight of mankind without recognizing its cause. The humanist works feverishly to free man from the effects of his unrecognized sinfulness, but not from sin itself. As a result he seeks remedies for its symptoms but does not perceive the disease and therefore ignores it. He caters to the pride of man and thus hastens man's downfall.

In the interest of clarity, what has been said is not to be equated with humanitarian concern, which is a fruit of Christianity. We are referring to humanism—a system of philosophy which regards the physical welfare, environment, and materials of man as his chief and only end. The humanist may effect a measure of change or reformation, but only Christ can redeem or cleanse. The new humanism —a syncretistic blend with Christianity—sees Christian ministry in terms of social action, not in terms of proclamation of sin and God's grace. The new humanism is a basic naturalistic heresy of our day, leading man to complacency, despair, defiance, and even to absurdity.

The new humanism looks at man as a "nice guy," and it overlooks and allows man's inconsistencies and errors. It contends that since we are not perfect, we must live with such tensions or ignore them and, possibly, someday we may get rid of them. This humanism treats man as if he were the lord of the world. This will bring no more success to the social order than can suicide to a better life. It destroys; it is a disintegrating force.

"Optimistic evolutionary humanism has no rational foundation," states Francis Schaeffer. "Its hope is always rooted in the leap of 'manana.' In looking for proof one is always diverted to tomorrow. This optimism is a leap, and we are foolish in our universities to be intimidated into thinking that the humanists have a rational basis for the 'optimistic' part of their slogan. They have not—they are irrational. . . . There is no God, according to Huxley, but we will say there is a God. . . . They are both involved in the leap. The mere use of religious words in contrast to nonreligious words changes nothing after the dichotomy and leap are accepted." [1]

The Feb. 26, 1962, Ghana *Evening News* printed a "Psalm of Dedication" for a self-declared humanist god, leader Kwame Nkrumah: "God doth magnify the savior, and his spirit rejoiced in Osagyefo. For his mercy is on them that fear evil. The Messiah has put down the greedy self-seekers from their seat and has exalted the humble. The deliverer has filled the hungry with good things, and provided the jobless with jobs. Oh, appear before Kwame with a new song of praise, for he has done marvelous things. . . . Kwame Nkrumah is truly great." Almost four years to the day after that blasphemous statement was printed, Kwame Nkrumah was deposed. God, in the words of Mary from which that psalm was taken, "put down the mighty from their throne." Even the statue of Nkrumah, announcing, "Seek ye first the political kingdom and all other things shall be added unto it," was destroyed. Another humanist government was put down.

Christianity has not failed, for it has not really been tried. In fact, only Christianity produces a real and proper "humanism." Naturalistic humanism leads to a diminish-

178

ing of man and eventually makes him a zero.

There is a viable alternative to the confusion and despair voiced by the humanist and contemporary man. This is the direct, existential, transforming relationship man can have with God by faith in Jesus Christ. It offers this relationship to the divine nature by a personal faith in the living Christ, the only means whereby fragmented human nature is actually made spiritually whole again (Col. 1:20-23). A person who has entered into this dynamic saving relationship with the Source of all authority, the Creator and Sustainer of the universe, will no longer find the humanist's views and theories tenable. Man is indeed dependent on God for moral values and truth, and is accountable to God. Christ's Gospel destroys the total sovereignty of man's reasoning powers and of a humanism that feeds on naturalistic philosophies.

C. S. Lewis reminds us that our world is "enemy-occupied territory." He said that Christianity is the story of how the rightful king has landed on earth in "disguise" and is calling on Christians to take part in a campaign of sabotage. Christians can never be comfortable with secular values.[2]

Christianity is a resistance movement, as thoughtful Christians stand together with Jesus to resist the world views that lead man down the road of dehumanization. True Christianity will not accept a church-humanism detente with the naturalistic educational systems and philosophies of this world.

When veteran linguistic missionary Eugene W. Bunkowske of Nigeria was asked, "How do you see the radical nature of Christianity over against other religions, philosophies, and movements in the world?" he said: "The well-known agnostic Herbert Spenser said that no man has ever been known to penetrate with his finite mind the veil that hides the mind of the Infinite. On this basis he concluded that the Infinite (God) may not be known by the finite (man). His statement reveals the essence of what the religions and philosophies of this world attempt to do. They want to find a way for man to reach God.

"Buddhism stretches for nirvana (passionless peace) through perfect self-control, unselfishness, knowledge, and enlightenment. Hinduism believes that the law of karma (good deeds) will lead man through the veil after many upward reincarnations. Islam teaches that prayer and kindness to others leads to eternal life. Traditional religions the world over attempt to reach spiritual power through sacrifice and the mediation of shrines, amulets, and charms. Even much so-called Christianity of our day operates on the basis that all truth must be discovered by man by investigating the natural order of existence.

"By its very nature Christianity is radically different. It never expects man to pierce the veil between the Infinite and the finite. Christianity rests on the premise that the Infinite (God) has taken the initiative and pierced the veil and come through to the finite (man). It is not that we have loved God, but that He loved us and sent His Son to be the means by which our sins are forgiven (1 John 4:10).

"Christianity is also radical in that, unlike the gods of the Greeks and other earthly religions who are often weak and selfish, it projects God as totally great, perfect, and powerful, but at the same time totally available and as near as Jesus: blessing the children, eating with publicans and sinners, healing the sick, preaching the Good News, choosing the disciples, and giving even the total sacrifice of Himself for the sins of all people. Christianity is unique in that it personalizes this nearness for every Christian. It delivers a new birth with a totally new dimension of life to all who are ready to say, "I believe." Christianity unites each believer with God as a son. This NEW LIFE gives a man something to live for, a cause to sacrifice for, and a special task to be perfected for.

"For me this spiritual union with God in Christ makes

each day new and exciting. It puts every experience, including suffering, doubt, prayer, temptation, joy, love, and even death, into a meaningful framework.

"It creates a basis for trust, respect, and love with my fellow human beings and leads me to realize that God, in fact, does work for good in all things 'with those who love Him, who are called according to His purpose' (Rom. 8:28 RSV).

"I have also had the wonderful privilege of seeing many here in Africa who have lived in fear and terror and continually attempted to appease the spirits through sacrifice receive God's free gift in Christ. What a joy to see the Holy Spirit eradicate fear and work His miracle of love and forgiveness in people who then progress on the basis of the spoken and written Word. This living Word is sharper than a two-edged sword. When accepted at face value, as seems so natural here in Africa, it cuts away the weight of sin, reforms lives and sharpens the human spirit for witness and works of love.

"Christianity is unique and radical because it works. It has real power, not 'man power' but 'God power,' not psychological gimicry but the gift of God's forgiveness and love which releases by the Holy Spirit the burdened human spirit for creative rebirth and meaningful association and response."

New Theology

Some theologians and churchmen, in their desire to make Christianity more meaningful to the humanistic and naturalistic world, have attempted to adapt Biblical truth to make it more palatable to the intellectuals, philosophers, scientists, and those who are offended by the supernatural elements in the Christian faith. They are so dedicated to the desire of making the Christian religion relevant to the supposed needs of modern man, so intent on constructing a "relevant" mission, that they consider it embarrassing and even a handicap to hold to the historic truths of Christianity which stress many supernatural acts in history itself. They want conformity to the extent that they advocate a synthesis, a merging of philosophic speculations and the Word of God. This, then, is the core of the "new theology."

The new theology, of course, is not really new at all, even though it offers only a few refinements of the old "liberal theology," to make it more palatable. The new theology is basically an attempt:

1) To relate God's redemptive deeds to history in such a way that there is no need to try to establish the *facts* of history. The "facts" of history may lie forever hidden under subjective interpretations, but this does not threaten theology so long as by the "leap of faith" we believe that on a level not subject to human investigation a divine purpose is being realized.

2) To relate (tell, speak about, proclaim) God's redemptive activity in theological formulas which because they are all ultimately only word-pictures of what God is doing may differ greatly from each other so long as *somehow* a divine, saving intent is expressed.

The new theology is characterized by the loss of the formal principle (the source from which all Christian teaching is derived and the standards by which it is judged) of "Scripture alone" and replacing it with whatever human authority and interpretation is at the moment in fashion. It reacts negatively to the historic Biblical heritage of the Christian church and reacts affirmatively to the currents of the times in the philosophical and ethical spheres. It offers "reconstruction" of Biblical truths instead of timely expositions of the facts of the text, and often adopts unproved assumptions and sets them up as the theological guides for the Church.

The spokesmen for the new theology often picture

themselves as present-day reformers of the church, appealing to the great Protestant principle that the church must always be reforming itself. This view perverts the nature and authority of the Scriptures. Every true reformation of the church has always worked in the direction of return to the truth of the Scriptures, not moving away from them. Of this Martin Luther is the prime exemplar. The new theologians offer a natural world without all of the supernatural elements of its Creator, an external present without a sure hereafter, a morality without absolute morals, a church without a sure Word, and subsequently a Savior whose words and Scripture are torn away from His Person.

The new theologians challenge the validity of the time-honored truths of Biblical inspiration and infallibility. They replace them with assumptions which propose a natural development of history exemplified in the Scriptures. Thus they are in tune with an evolutionary approach to the study of the Bible.

Naturalism has been the heart of Biblical criticism from the day of Wellhausen until now, for the miraculous and the supernatural are ruled out. Naturalism is applied also to Israel's history. The interpretations are made dependent on literary devices arbitrarily pressed into use to change fact into fiction. As was to be expected, deviations were proposed which set one interpretation against another. The authority of the Word was discarded for the presuppositions, speculations, and pronouncements of individuals or groups enveloped in the evolutionist's orbit.

This neo-Christianity has crept like a paralysis through various churches and destroyed their spiritual power. The system of interpretation itself is not a minor perversion of the Christian faith, but a religion with opposing dogmas and beliefs. Artificial criteria are applied, which both logic and the Scripture must reject. We are asked to substitute a hypothetical reconstruction for the authentic Word.

A typical example is a book by the deceased James Pike, advertised as telling "what to keep—not what to throw out," putting into a positive statement the same thing which should be stated negatively. So we find Pike coming back to his pulpit at St. John the Divine in New York observing: "It was from this pulpit that I forged and worked through my attempts to bring the church, though kicking and screaming, into the modern world." The church became the mouthpiece of scholars and their students instead of the voice of God. Who were these pastors and professors speaking for? Certainly not God!

Theologians of this kind give the impression that most of the world would like to become Christian if only theology would be modernized. That is a cruel delusion. This theology is simply man's art of making the Bible say what man wants to hear, which affects the great mission of God negatively.

Culture-Christianity

Some of the new theology merely absorbs the spirit of the age or the culture. The church has always been tempted to merge with the world. Theology as a human enterprise is subject to such human exposition corrupted by original sin.

"Culture-Christianity" seeks to love both the secular and the sacred without defining the antitheses between them. It was the root of the problem with the Corinthians, who sought the wisdom of words, walked after the manner of men, and glorified man. However, God offers a Gospel in conflict with man and culture—a message of Christ crucified. The Corinthians dramatized the ease with which the human mind can take offense at the Gospel and turn it into something acceptable to human beings. At the same time, the thorns of absolutism and uniqueness are pruned away in the interest of acceptability in the greenhouse of culture. The new theology which is a reflection of the culture in which it lives is merely a human-ology.[3]

One uniqueness of Christianity is that it may be clothed in the forms and expressions of any culture without compromise. However, it always brings a supernatural dimension into the culture, and it challenges any and all sinful aspects of the culture. Christian presuppositions and doctrine are not to be weakened or rejected for the sake of naturalistic assumptions and presuppositions inherent in human culture.

Culture-Christianity makes the church a thermometer that registers rather than a thermostat that regulates. It may be named an IBM theology which registers all the factors in the current situation and reflects a general consensus. Who decides what is right? The tribe of new theologians in every new consensus.

Culture-Christianity is like a scientist, first checking public opinion, then proceeding on the assumptions of majority opinion—or like a doctor asking relatives about the advisability of surgery on a patient. It is accommodation of the church to the world. If the church has been entrusted with the plan of salvation and the eternal Word of God, the relevance of Christianity is automatically established. To try to impose on it any other standard of relevance is wrong.

There is no way to bridge or overcome the enmity between the church and the world, for the Christian or the church cannot accept conformity to the world in an effort to help the world. Doing so would be a betrayal of Christ and the world. C. H. Spurgeon asked: "Do you imagine that the Gospel is a nose of wax, which can be shaped to suit the face of each succeeding age? If the revelation once given by the Spirit of God is to be interpreted according to the fashion of the period, then the witness of the Holy Spirit is shaped and molded at our will."

Biblical research is not the problem (for it is a necessity); the problem lies with the researchers. Some are like the Athenians in the day of Paul, who "spent their time in nothing else but either to tell or to hear something new" (Acts 17:21). They read each other's books, quote each other's questions or denials of the Christian faith, and end up with little more to offer than a basket of opinions. Though some of the culture-oriented theologians have betrayed their trust, they still want to be trusted. Some call the disturbance caused by their accommodation a "lover's quarrel with the church," but what they are doing is spiritual adultery, as Francis Schaeffer, quoting the Scriptures, calls it. Biblical scholarship, he points out, is quoted, instead of the Bible itself. Doubt is presented as a virtue, with the result that the unwary become engulfed in human opinions and ignorance. As to the propagating scholars, they seem to be embarrassed whenever they are confronted with a strict commitment and confession of historic Biblical truth.

When any interpretation contradicts the plain statements of the Scriptures, we know that such interpretation is not of God. Wherever the doctrine of inspiration and the authority of the Bible are relativized or downgraded (no matter how orthodox a group may be on other points), spiritual decay is inevitable. For then contradictory divergencies become merely exploratory questions. Those who hold implicitly to the clear meaning of God's Word against modern scholarship are labeled "obscurantist."

We would be more than foolish if we ditched our historic Christian beliefs, which have sustained us, simply because a large segment of so-called "mainstream Christianity" has succumbed to doubt, speculation, and sometimes even to despair. What is so terrifyingly tragic is that these victims have lost their realization of the supernatural destiny which God's love has set for man. Instead of planting the Seed, they cut it in pieces in their studies. R. A. Torrey once said that if some Bible interpreters "were practicing law and should try in any court of justice to interpret law as they interpret the Bible, they would be laughed out of court." [4]

Church history shows that when church members have drifted from a solid commitment to Biblical truths, the "Good News" becomes mere pious talk, forever theorizing about Christ, and the members lose their zeal for evangelism and missions. On the other hand, wherever the authority and trustworthiness of the Scriptures are accepted faithfully without reservations, a church can survive quarrels and even temporary error on some points because the Scriptures will eventually make the necessary corrections and straighten such matters out.

Syncretism Dilutes and Destroys the Christian Faith

The lordship of Jesus Christ calls for total, unreserved acceptance of Jesus Christ as the absolute and only Savior of all. The command of God is to pull down every idol, whether it is found in Jerusalem, Athens, Tokyo, Calcutta, or New York. Rather than taking good points from heathen religions and trying to fuse them with Christianity, vain idols need to be destroyed.[5]

Though it is true the world over, as Paul tells us in Romans 1 and 2, that man feels responsible to God, it is equally true that the natural and traditional worship of man is the result of his total depravity. The religious worshiper whose God is not the Christ of the Scriptures must be rescued from dumb idols to serve the living God. It is not mere cultural pride, but the Christian's conviction of his responsibility, to tell the sinner wherever he is that he is dead in trespasses and sins. This is true of the entire human race throughout all of human history since the historic fall of Adam and Eve.[6]

The witnessing Christian will protest all ideas in the world which conflict with the general truths of God's Word. To accept what he finds in a given culture without question is to make peace with a sub-Biblical, humanistic religious system. All values which include self-interest and self-support, that deny the need for supernatural powers, should be rejected. Syncretism cuts out the radical quality of Christianity and tends to make of the church a comfortable institution for those who have the inclination to enjoy it.

The New Universalism

Dr. Jack McAlister, president of World Literature Crusade, asked his radio audience for a response to the question: "Do you believe the heathen are lost?" Amazingly, 26% of the responders (apparently Christian listeners) answered that they did not believe the heathen are lost. Various statements were sent that were rationalizations, emotional arguments, humanistic philosophies, but not Biblical fact to back up that false notion.

Even though the center of the current theological storm is the authority and nature of the Scriptures, the *Gospel itself* is at stake. The great mission of our Lord is vitally affected by this debate, for it touches the chief Scriptural doctrine of "justification by faith." Only recently have we been aware that voices raised in favor of lowered views of the Scriptures are often tied to a new "Christological" universalism as distinguished from the old humanistic universalism of the Unitarian Universalists.

The "new universalism" is a "Christian" or "Christological" universalism which holds to objective justification, but not to subjective justification. Objective justification means that Christ in His redemptive act has paid for the salvation of all people, for through Christ's sacrifice on the cross God has been reconciled to all men. Subjective justification means that man receives the benefits of Christ's redemptive act *only through faith in Jesus* and thus becomes reconciled to God.

The new universalism or neo-universalism builds its case on the fact of objective justification, but it ignores the individual or subjective question of faith through

188

which man appropriates eternal salvation. "Christological" universalism, which opens heaven to those who did not have an opportunity, holds that it is the business of Christians and the church to bring to the attention of all that God has given them a new humanity through Christ. This new humanity is to be demonstrated and celebrated so that men become aware of their salvation.

A natural feeling of compassion for the lost ones causes some people to attempt to find loopholes or to rationalize the situation so that a way is left open for salvation to those who have never heard of Christ and have never had an opportunity. Some believe that God is not obliged to carry out His threats and justice. Others lean on God's quality of love and compassion, but fail to stress His justice. Some trust that God's steadfast love is greater than His holiness, and they leave it to God because they know that they can trust Him to show love. They argue that our understanding is incomplete. Many sincerely question how it is possible that a person could be condemned when he never had an opportunity to hear of Christ before he died. Others will argue that those who earnestly seek God might somehow be saved.

In contrast, the Scriptures say that only the righteous and the regenerated may enter heaven. Unrighteous and unregenerate man will be excluded from heaven and will be condemned to eternal damnation. This righteousness is gained through faith in Jesus: "His faith is counted for righteousness" (Rom. 4:5); "they were ignorant of God's righteousness and went about trying to establish their own righteousness; but righteousness is for everyone that believes" (Rom. 10:3-4). The Gospel of Christ does not provide automatic salvation for everyone, but only for everyone that *believes*.[7]

Special attention needs to be given to the *exclusive terms* which separate the believer completely from the merits of his own works, and gives salvation by *grace* (free gift) *alone*, and by *faith alone* in Christ. When St. Paul says, "We hold that a man is justified by faith apart from works of law" (Rom. 3:28 RSV), some people are offended by the particle "alone"; however, we also face the exclusive particle "alone" in the other exclusive terms which the New Testament uses with salvation, namely, "freely . . . not of works . . . it is a gift." God shows that He requires repentance and faith, a turning from wicked ways and a life through faith in God (Ezek. 33:11).

The punishment and penalty of sin is death, eternal damnation together with other bodily, spiritual, temporal, and eternal misery. This inherited guilt is so great and terrible that in believers alone can it be covered up for Jesus' sake and forgiven before God.

Few Scriptural texts are clearer than 2 Thessalonians 1:7-10 to show that faith is necessary for salvation, and that condemnation is due those who do not believe the Gospel: "When the Lord Jesus is revealed from heaven with His mighty angels in flaming fire, inflicting vengeance upon those who do not know God and upon those who do not obey the Gospel of our Lord Jesus. They shall suffer the punishment of eternal destruction and exclusion from the presence of the Lord and from the glory of His might, when He comes on that day to be glorified in His saints, and to be marveled at in all who have believed, because our testimony to you was believed." (RSV)

The Lutheran Confessions are confessions of faith that have for 400 years described the witness of many Reformation believers. They affirm: "These Articles of the Creed, therefore, divide and distinguish us Christians from all other people on earth. All who are outside the Christian church, whether heathen, Turks, Jews, false Christians and hypocrites . . . remain in eternal wrath and damnation, for they do not have the Lord Jesus, and, besides, they are not illuminated and blessed by the gifts of the Holy Spirit".[8] "The trouble is that their [the heathen] trust is false and wrong, for it is not founded upon the one God, apart from whom there is truly no god in heaven or on earth." [9]

The Athanasian Creed is very clear: "Whoever wishes to be saved must, above all else, hold the true Christian faith. Whoever does not keep it whole and undefiled will without doubt perish for eternity. . . . It is also necessary for eternal salvation that one faithfully believe that our Lord Jesus Christ became man, for this is the right faith, that we believe and confess that the Lord Jesus Christ, the Son of God, is at once God and man. . . . Unless a man believe this firmly and faithfully, he cannot be saved." [10]

Some argue that it is only those who *reject* Jesus that are damned, but that those who do not believe merely because they have never had an opportunity to hear of Christ may be able to escape the condemnation. It is not only unbelief that damns, or only he who believes not that is damned, but also he who has never heard of Christ and thus lacks saving faith is also without hope and under God's condemnation for time and eternity.

If there would be any truth to the idea that a heathen, an Indian, a Nigerian, or an American, who has never heard or known Christ in his life will not go to hell under the condemnation of his sins, we would have to come to the conclusion that it is quite superfluous to send missionaries overseas, for God will somehow save the heathen anyway, but particularly unnecessary because we know that of all people who hear and learn of Christ, almost three-fourths of them will refuse to believe. Therefore, on this basis, these three-fourths will go to hell and be damned (that is, if we at least believe that "he who believeth not shall be damned"). If this view is valid, we must contrive a new kind of Gospel and a new standard of salvation and damnation — in total contradiction to the Scriptures.

Rather than setting ourselves up as judges of the compassion and love of God by questioning Scriptural truths or by presenting theories in contradiction to what God's

Word teaches, we ought to weep for our own failures in reaching the three of the four billion now living on earth who do not confess Christ. We ought to be part of a group which some participants at the Lausanne Congress on World Evangelization called "the Company of the Broken-hearted." However, we shall not only stop at being broken-hearted over this tragic situation, but also be motivated by Christ's great love for all and for us in having brought us to saving faith by the Holy Spirit.

Universalism does not conform to the full testimony of the Bible and must be rejected. It cannot be supported from the Scriptures and is a heresy. To be sure, the Scriptures proclaim a universal redemption wrought by the Lord Jesus Christ. But this, the Scriptures also proclaim, must be accepted through faith in Jesus Christ, the world's only Savior. The Holy Spirit's gift of faith through the hearing of the Gospel (objective and historical) is the only means whereby Christ's substitutionary life and death are imputed to man for justification unto eternal life.

God has ordained that man shall come to know that he has been saved when the Holy Spirit calls him with the Gospel message, spelled out for him in the Holy Scriptures. With this message the Holy Spirit works faith in man's heart, enlightens Him with His gifts, and keeps him in the true faith. Everyone who rejects the salvation wrought for him by Christ will be eternally damned. Faith in Jesus makes the difference.

All people who ever lived on earth will stand before the Judgment Seat of Christ on the Last Day, and their faith or unfaith will determine their eternal destiny. If there have been 10 billion people who have had breath on earth by that time, then 10 billion people will not escape the scrutiny of God's justice, which will be satisfied only by faith in Christ's atoning sacrifice on Calvary. Although there will be thousands of ethnic and tribal groups before the Judgment Seat, they will all be divided into only two groups: (1) those "guilty" as charged; (2) those "not guilty," their guilt forgiven and removed by Christ.

Christians need to be more aggressive and faithful in obedience to the Savior's Great Commission, and participate in an all-out strategy for reaching the entire world of lost people in our lifetime.

Faith and Reason

Christianity is a supernatural religion which cannot be secularized or flattened out into a religion-in-general without denying its very nature and rejecting its world mission. When it is reduced to something satisfactory to the unregenerate mind and heart, it is no longer Christianity and it has lost its radical mission. There is only one way the Bible could be the Book for all men of all ages — the supernatural way. The Holy Spirit Himself is the real Author of the Book. "For we did not follow cleverly devised myths. . . . We have the prophetic Word made more sure" (2 Peter 1:16, 19 RSV).

God's Word is its own proof for its reliability. We do not need archaeology to prove the Bible is correct. It is a fact that the Bible contains hundreds, possibly thousands, of historical and geographical points which have been tested by archaeology and found to be accurate, as point after point in the Old and New Testaments has been substantiated by archaeological findings. Nowhere in other religious literature are we introduced to people with details of their daily lives such as are found in the Bible. Yet we do not use archaeology to prove that the Bible is true. However, in the hands of those who use it properly, archaeology is a means of understanding the Biblical age. It has added support to the written record, but it does not add anything to faith. It serves to show that the Scriptures are credible, trustworthy, and reliable in matters of history and custom. What it confirms are the material things, not the spiritual content. The Bible is the Word of God because God inspired it, not because archaeology has demonstrated its historical accuracy.

Honest scholarship will refuse to adopt two points of view which are diametrically opposed or to try to synthesize truth with error. In his *The God Who Is There*, Francis Schaeffer supplies a historical background for our present theological problem. He says that it was the German philosopher Hegel who became the first man to open the door to the line of despair. Before his time, truth was conceived on the basis of the antitheses, relating to the idea of cause and effect. Hegel's answer was synthesis, which changed the world to try to live with compromise rather than to accept or reject one point of view or the other.[11]

Schaeffer states that if we use reason operating with the thesis-antithesis-synthesis method, we shall have nothing left to say and will stand for nothing. Christianity may still keep its outward institutional form and words, but it will all become abstract and impersonal. Then Christianity has the marks of death upon it, and it will soon be one more museum piece. The old liberal theologians in Germany accepted the uniformity of natural causes and rejected the miraculous and supernatural. They were doomed to failure, for the supernatural is so intertwined with all else that without it there is no Jesus left. Schaeffer further indicates that the phrase "Jesus Christ" has become a contentless banner that can be carried in any direction for sociological purposes.

Contributing more insights in his *Escape from Reason*, Schaeffer observes that the new theologians went adrift with synthesis, where there is no truth and no nontruth in antithesis, no right and no wrong. He says that Jesus turned out to be a nondefined symbol. They use the word because it is rooted in the memory of the race. It is humanism with a religious banner called "Jesus," to which they can give any content they wish, Schaeffer asserts.

The entire Bible leads us to believe that it is impossible

194

to have faith in a person without accepting facts about that person. Faith involves the acceptance of the Scriptural declarations about Christ and His entire Word. The book *Christ: The Theme of the Bible* shows the authority, integrity, and unity of the Bible, especially in its historical parts. Author Geisler says: "There are numerous individual citations which reveal that Jesus affirmed an authoritative collection of writings, divine in origin, and unimpeachable in their declarations. Compare, for example, the fact that (1) Jesus resisted Satan by three emphatic quotations of the Old Testament prefaced by 'it is written' (Matt. 4:4, 7, 10). (2) Jesus cleansed the temple on the authority that 'It is written, My house shall be called a house of prayer' (Matt. 21:13). (3) He pronounced a woe on His betrayer, based on the fact that 'it is written' (Matt. 26:24). (4) Jesus rebuked religious hypocrisy, with 'as it is written' (quoting Is. 29:13 in Mark 7:6). (5) He affirmed His own Messiahship from 'the place where it was written, The Spirit of the Lord is upon me . . .' (Luke 4:17-18). (6) Jesus answered the lawyer's question on how to inherit eternal life by saying, 'What is written in the law?' (Luke 10:26). (7) He based His own authority and identity with God on the basis of the fact that 'it is written in the prophets' (John 6:45; cf. 10:34). (8) Jesus even affirmed the authority of what was written (in the Old Testament) despite the fact that the religious authorities of His day wished to kill Him for it (cf. Luke 20:16-17)." [12]

Geisler continues: "Furthermore, with regard to the canonization and authentication of the Old Testament by Christ, there can be no question that Jesus was not an accommodator. Jesus never hesitated to rebuke existing religious views that were not true, as He did to the Jews who exalted their 'traditions' above 'God's commandments' (Matt. 15:1-3). Six times in the Sermon on the Mount, He contrasted His affirmations with false Jewish interpretations of the Old Testament, in such phrases as 'you have heard that it was said . . . but I say unto you' (Matt. 5:21-22, 27-28, 31-32, 33-34, 38-39, 43-44). Jesus often told them, as in Matt. 22:29, 'You are wrong, because you know neither the Scriptures nor the power of God.'

". . . Christ's verification of the historical character of Old Testament events. Jesus personally verified the historical truth of (1) Adam and Eve (Matt. 19:4); (2) Abel's murder (Matt. 23:35); (3) Noah and the Flood (Luke 17:27); (4) Lot and the destruction of Sodom (Luke 17:29); (5) the existence of the patriarchs Abraham, Isaac, and Jacob (Luke 13:28); (6) Moses and the burning bush (Luke 20:37); (7) the wilderness wanderings of Israel (John 3:14); (8) the story of Elijah and the widow (Luke 4:25); (9) and of Naaman the Syrian leper (Luke 4:27); (10) David and the tabernacle (Matt. 12:3-4); (11) Solomon and the queen of Sheba (Matt. 12:42); (12) Jonah and Nineveh (Matt. 12:41); and (13) Daniel the prophet (Matt. 24:15).

". . . Christ's verification of the miraculous character of Old Testament events. The events of the Old Testament were not only considered to be historical but many of them were also supernatural in character. In effect, Jesus' references verify the miraculous nature of Old Testament events:

1. The world's destruction by a flood (Luke 17:27)
2. Lot's wife being crystallized (Luke 17:32)
3. The burning bush before Moses (Luke 20:37)
4. The healing of Israel from snakebites (John 3:14)
5. The manna from heaven (John 6:49)
6. The healing of Naaman the leper (Luke 4:26)
7. The miracles of Elijah for the widow (Luke 4:25)
8. The preservation of Jonah in the big fish (Matt. 12:41)." [13]

The Gospel is denied in a substantial way if we deny Jonah as historical, when Jesus uses that account as predictive of His resurrection. The Gospel is denied in a substantial manner if we deny the Flood, when it is used as predictive of the power of the Word in destroying the earth by fire on Judgment Day (2 Peter 3:6-7). It was the confidence in the historical record of Dwight Eisenhower that gave the majority of American people confidence in the ability and record of Eisenhower to elect him their President. John F. Kennedy would not have been elected President if a majority of the people would not have had trust in his ability and beliefs based on his actual record in war and peace. It is untenable to tear history and the truths it teaches apart, whether it is Eisenhower and Kennedy or whether it is Christ, John, Abraham, or Moses.

Paul's defense and faith in Acts 20:1-19 are built on historical facts, as he presents them not as inspiring allegories but as accurate historical accounts with a divine purpose.

The "new theology" brings with it a repudiation of the supernatural and miraculous. But if one link of the miraculous is broken, then all links are broken. If Christ was born of a virgin, if Christ rose from dead, then Israel passed through the Red Sea on dry land and was fed by manna from heaven in the wilderness, then Genesis 1 and 2 is history as God wants us to know it, then regeneration and the indwelling Christ are a reality, then the power of the Holy Spirit through the Word is available to win the world for Christ. The question is whether a person will have faith in Christ on a humanistic or on a Scriptural basis.

Proponents of the new theology sometimes offer false options. We isolate several that are unacceptable:

1. They offer a false option between Christ and the Bible. When we confess God's Word to be the inerrant, infallible written Word in the historical sense, some strongly criticize us of being guilty of Bibliolatry or Biblicism. Christ and the Bible are not antitheses. Recall the quotations from Geisler's book. He emphasized: "You

cannot separate the authority of Christ from the authority of the written Scriptures which reveal Christ." Some maintain that those who believe the Bible to be an errorless and infallible Source are worshiping the Bible. What should concern us more is idolatry—idolizing man's mind and his own notions.

2. Another false option is proposed between God's Word and love. Those who believe God's Word demands certain norms and evangelical discipline are sometimes considered legalistic and devoid of love. Luther says that the sins against doctrine are worse than those against love, that the first is committed against the Word and Christian faith, and the second against love. The sin against doctrine is in no wise to be tolerated, but we are to have patience with sin against love because by it we sin only against our neighbor without violating doctrine and faith. Luther writes: "Therefore we shall let them enlarge on concord and Christian love, while we shall rather enlarge on the majesty of the Word and faith. It behooves love to bear all and yield to everyone. However, it behooves faith . . . to yield to no one." [14]

Love honors God's Word. Love is the fulfilling of the Law, not the breaking of it. Those who know Christian love will heed God's Word even when it is unpopular—and when some pit love against God's Word. Jesus demands right belief, which we learn only from God's Word, which in turn teaches and produces Christian love.

3. An unfortunate option suggested by some is that we must change our message or lose our youth, students, and intellectuals. This is wrongly identifying the nature of the problem. Man doesn't want to hear what God's Word has to say. The question is the same as at Paul's time in Athens: Why were the results of Paul's powerful and magnificent address on Mars' Hill so meager? The reason was not in the

nature or method of the presentation, nor was it in Paul, but in the Athenians. In the case of Jesus Himself from the Gospels we see that "He could not do many mighty works there because of their unbelief," and so we would not say the cause was in the impotency of Christ, but in the hardness and unbelief of His listeners. The "Athenian University" was the home of the cool, cultivated, critical intellect, which had tried all things and found all wanting, and so few hearers had open ears for Paul's new teaching. The Gospel, though an offense to man's wisdom, must not be changed.

In a day when absolutes are questioned or rejected by many, we should remind ourselves of the highly technical and successful community that sends the missiles and astronauts to the moon, people who demand precision in every detail for the safety of the workers and the success of their mission. Truth is absolute. We insist that our druggist must work by absolutes, for our lives depend on it. The purpose and enjoyment of athletic contests are completely destroyed if there are no absolute rules and regulations, or if the referee does not follow them. Boating will be disastrous if the pilot does not use absolutes.

The same is true in the realm of religion, for the historical Christ Himself is an absolute. Though He were born a thousand times in Bethlehem, if He is not born in my heart by faith, His gift of salvation has been rejected and I am lost eternally. That's a Biblical absolute.

We are not discussing fake images of Christ—the church's "Christ," a theologian's "Christ," but the Christ of the written Word. He is very exclusive. Most *exclusive* are the statements He made regarding the way of salvation and the path of faith here on earth. But He is also inclusive in that He shed His blood for all men, for He paid the *inclusive* price for all people's salvation. Yet He becomes exclusive when faith is demanded for the acceptance of the gift of salvation (Eph. 2:8-10).

Paul says that we are not to be "carried away with different and strange doctrines" (Heb. 13:9). Also: "For I have not shunned to declare unto you all the counsel of God. . . . After my departing shall grievous wolves enter in among you, not sparing the flock. Also of your own selves shall men arise, speaking perverse things, to draw away disciples after them. Therefore watch, and remember that by the space of three years I ceased not to warn everyone night and day with tears" (Acts 20:27-32). "Take heed unto yourself, and unto the doctrine; continue in them: for in doing this you shall both save yourself and them that hear you" (1 Tim. 4:16).

God warns: "First, I want to remind you that in the last days there will come scoffers who will do every wrong they can think of, and laugh at the truth. . . . 'As far back as anyone can remember everything has remained exactly as it was since the first day of creation.' They deliberately forget this fact: that God did destroy the world with a mighty flood, long after he had made the heavens by the word of His command, and had used the waters to form the earth and surround it. And God has commanded that the earth and the heaven be stored away for a great bonfire at the judgment day, when all ungodly men will perish" (2 Peter 3:3-7 Living Bible). "Oh, Timothy, don't fail to do these things that God entrusted to you. Keep out of foolish arguments with those who boast of their 'knowledge' and thus prove their lack of it. Some of these people have missed the most important thing in life — they don't know God" (1 Tim. 6:20-21 Living Bible). "Remind your people of these great facts, and command them in the name of the Lord not to argue over unimportant things. Such arguments are confusing and useless, and even harmful. Steer clear of foolish discussions which lead people into the sin of anger with each other" (2 Tim. 2:14, 16 Living Bible).

The faithful Christian interpreter on Christ's mission will reject the following views and practices: 1. Coordinating the Scriptures with church tradition; 2. Placing any authority or scholarship above the Scriptures; 3. Viewing the Scriptures as the record of the natural evolution of the faith of Israel and the early church; 4. Viewing the prophetic and apostolic Word as no more than a unique but fallible, human witness to revelation; 5. Failing to acknowledge the organic unity and essential Christocentricity of the Old and New Testaments; 6. Going beyond the "plain sense" of the Scriptures by means of allegorical or existential interpretation; 7. Failing to hear the Scriptures on their own terms and their own categories by the attempt to make them conform to a preconceived system of thought; 8. Abusing the recognition that the Scriptures employ various literary genres by arbitrarily classifying certain sections of the Scriptures as myths or legends—a rather unscholarly procedure.

New Morality

The "new theology" breeds the "new morality" and an untenable situational ethics. Christian faith and Biblical truth have a quality of constancy and continuity which is denied by the relativism of the new morality. Disappearance of religious absolutes has encouraged man to deify himself and pamper himself. As man takes the reins of life and destiny into his own hands, he adopts standards of ethics and morality from his unregenerate heart. Establishing man as a worthy authority means the disestablishment of God. This humanistic position is unrealistic, for it does not take proper account of the existence of evil and the absolute depravity of human nature. In humanist thinking, a person must not think in moral or ethical absolutes and accept any extrahuman source of power or standard in acknowledging and understanding right and wrong. The new morality views a man's life as restricted to his consciousness of the human situation, making him a prisoner of sinful nature. This offers no hope to the confused and weak, as they are defeated by their own emotional conflicts and wanton desires.

The ethical crisis today centers in the refusal to acknowledge God's law as His eternal and immutable will, and to acknowledge sin as man's rebellion against the Law.

Unscriptural ethics and the new morality have attributes that look down to man, rather than up to God. Our society has grown so accustomed to encourage people to go their own way without the slightest reference to the will of God that some of the gravest aberrations are condoned. Several generations now have been brought up on the new morality, screamed at them by rock bands, taught by teachers and professors in schools, and heard and seen in movies, drama, and television.

The harvest of this moral permissiveness is seen in depleted morals, chaos, confusion, and personal destruction. What started out as a hunt for the good and happy life has ended in humiliation, loneliness, hatred, guilt complexes, a suicidal plunge, and death. Abortion is thus not only declared desirable for society, but faithful Christians are even to be taxed to pay for abortion on demand. Meanwhile, VD clinics are maintained so that extramarital sex can continue to be enjoyed and encouraged.

When people get a failing grade in dogma, Law and Gospel, we cannot expect more than an F in morals. The new morality makes personal self-satisfaction the criterion for acceptable human behavior. It is an individualism which lacks social concern for others and personal respect for one's self. It advances the notion that nothing is really wrong so long as nobody gets hurt. Heartache and pain have been experienced by people who have been lured into the playboy philosophy in life, ending with broken dreams, shattered ideals, and sick consciences.

Ingredients that lend support to the new morality are

irresponsible parents, a nontheistic national educational system, mass media dominated by violence, and religious leaders who have lost their way. These give birth to corruption, pornography, violence, lawlessness, immorality, and rebellion.

The world needs to learn what Christians know: There is a law of cause and effect, as seen in Romans 1:18-32, which reveals a frightful descending of moral steps of beliefs and action. The Scriptures tell us that God's Word should be plain to men, but some do not allow the truth to shape their belief and life. They become vain in their imagination, their thoughts become nonsense, and they indulge in futile speculation (v. 21). Behind a facade of wisdom, they become fools (v. 22). They change the glory of the incorruptible God into images made to look like corruptible men (v. 23). God's Word describes the process of human corruption taking place in our day. The results are revealed in v. 24: God gives them up to do the filthy things their hearts desire. They change God's truth into a lie, and they make more of material life than the Creator (v. 25). They reverence the things made instead of the Maker. God then gives people up to vile affections and actions—perverted use of sex (v. 26-27). Since they refuse to keep in mind the true knowledge about God, He gives them over to their corrupt and depraved minds (v. 28). They become deceitful and proud, and they give approval to unnatural and wrong things.

The cause and result of Scriptural perversion and lack of love of truth is shown in 2 Thessalonians 2:11: "For this cause God shall send them strong delusion, that they should believe a lie." Such strong religious delusions have been proclaimed in many forms since the apostolic age, when delusions were preached by Judaizers, Gnostics, and Montanists. Following centuries had their Manicheans, Donatists, Arians, Pelagians, and others. Since the 1800s Europe has given birth to many systems of theologies, and America is a producer of "new" things in religion. Most of them are old heresies revived in new form. Truly, the new theology leads to the new morality.

The Natural and Supernatural in Science

1. Science

Science is a wonderful gift of God, and is man's opportunity to discern principles and laws which God made for man in the world. Science is the discovery of facts by observations and experiments to develop theories that can be tested and used. Science speaks to the *what* and *how*, matters that are observable *now*. It is not a sufficient guide for philosophy and life. It helps discover and produce many things beneficial to living, but always works under limitations.

Accelerated changes in life and scientific knowledge make some think that certain Christian beliefs must be replaced, whereas it is much of past scientific belief that is being revised regularly: check it in school science textbooks of 30, 15, and 5 years ago—and then today's texts. Much of science is temporary, subject to great revision regularly. Many scientists, in fact, are constantly telling us not to deify science.

The concern of Christians is the *natural* and *supernatural*. The scientist seeks natural explanations (physical phenomena). Through God's Word Christians can find supernatural explanations. The two are not even explanations of the same things, much less from the same point of view. The scientist deliberately excludes the supernatural from his studies because the supernatural is outside his ability to measure. For that reason he cannot be led to the same view of creation as Genesis presents; he has no way of investigating spiritual explanations and values. The validity of God's Word does not depend on how much it corresponds with scientific theories.

Science may provide some insights to indicate God has walked our way, but it is absurd for any scientist to turn naturalistic theory into "Thus saith the Lord." Scientists should be the ones who according to St. Paul discern in nature the glory of God. But instead of seeing the abundant evidences of His special design, some become "vain in their imagination" (Rom. 1:20-21).

A Christian view of science recognizes the excellence of science and its description of the physical world, but it also recognizes a severe limitation in not being able to reconstruct beginnings. Modern man is imprisoned in space, time, and matter, and he has no capacity to respond to any supernatural mode of external reality. It is especially regrettable that naturalistic assumptions pitted against the Biblical record meet us on every side, even from the mouths of theologians. C. S. Lewis said: "We all have Naturalism in our bones and even conversion does not at once work the infection out of our system. Its assumptions rush back upon the mind the moment viligance is relaxed. . . . [Church scholars] make it part of their method to eliminate the supernatural wherever it is even remotely possible to do so, to strain natural explanation even to the breaking point before they admit the least suggestion of miracle." [15]

God is not a natural phenomenon. He is Spirit, and He can be known only by faith. Christ is "both the first principle and the upholding principle of the whole scheme of creation" (Col. 1:17 Phillips). God not only brings all things into existence, but He also continually "upholds all things by the Word of His power" (Heb. 1:3). There is one single reality in the total scheme of things, and the Christian faith displays that reality. The whole universe is but a witness to God's power.

2. Science and Evolution

The new theology produces the demand to accept

theistic evolution as a viable option for the doctrine of creation in the Bible. Evolutionistic hypotheses have never been established by true science as a law or fact. Science has three classifications of ideas: hypotheses, theories, and laws. Evolution is a hypothesis, not an established fact. Darwin's *Origin of Species* is said to have 800 phrases like "Hence . . . let us suppose . . . it may be . . . let us conclude," etc., but others, nevertheless, have distorted these hypotheses into a religious conviction.

Some have shown the impossibility of the survival of various animals, insects, birds, and fish if evolution is to be taken seriously. Behind the existence of life on land and in the oceans is a master plan based on a unique series of food chains that preserve and sustain all of life on earth, and they are completely interdependent. There is a fantastic web in life of interdependence and absolute necessity of standard conditions if certain plants, birds, animals, or fish are to survive even for five minutes. Only a supernatural Power could produce these conditions. There are no intermediate steps possible.

Evolution as generally understood is more than change; it assumes certain kinds or series of changes resulting in the development of many, many life forms. It is based on the assumption of unchanging rates (uniformity), thus avoiding the supernatural. Evolution misses the fact that genetic variations are within rigidly fixed limits.

Onetime events, such as the world's beginning, cannot be proved or disproved by science. The proofs of science depend on "repeatability." Only one scientist was present at the earth's origin—and His name is God. He asked Moses to record the findings of His laboratory work in Genesis. No one can back up time in order to place in that Creation laboratory a contemporary scientist who might measure or test the beginnings experimentally. Man's partial observations from hindsight do not affect God's original record.

Evolutionary propositions are generalizations based on observations and are to be classified as such. They are a system of thought—not history but a "philosophy." No fallen creature can explain those beginnings; no one dare tell God to change days to eons, miracles to modified natural events. Great disagreement is found in the theories about the world's age, while some maneuver illogically to change the meaning of "day" in Genesis and Exodus— or the connotation of "evening and morning" making a day.

The second law of thermodynamics insists on a universal tendency toward decay and disorder, not growth and development as evolutionary theories claim. The Bible tells about the fact and reason for decay after creation. This decay will not last forever.[16]

Animals, fowl, or fish could not survive without complete reproductive functions, for no intermediate steps would allow them to survive. Sperm must be produced in the necessary channels for their mating. Timing, maturity, campatibility, balance—all must be just right in order that the new life might be formed. And what about the working of the eye, the balance nerve, the blood system, or the brain? Evolution of these organs is a biological and philosophical impossibility. And yet some Christian theologians seek to baptize the evolutionary theory and name it theistic evolution—as if God started the whole process by creating a few cells and then letting them develop.

The embryo of any living organism grows according to design, but the evolution theory cannot account for such intelligent direction and organization, whereas the Bible can. The fertilized egg cell contains in its tiny nucleus not only all the genetic instructions for building a human body, but also a complete manual on how to construct the complex protective housing that makes possible the embryo's existence. Evolution cannot account for that marvelous and intricate process. Not a single step in the evolutionary mechanism has been properly clarified.

207

Scientists who construct a world view on the basis of evolution are stating their religious beliefs or unbeliefs rather than proved conclusions from scientific investigations. The evolutionary theory does not make it easier to believe God's Word. The consensus of scientific opinion—whatever that may be in any age—is not a trustworthy guide for interpreting the Bible. Most of the tensions between science and Christianity have resulted from a partial understanding or misunderstanding of the problem.

3. *The Bible*

The doctrine of creation is not an obscure doctrine: There are 65 Old Testament passages that are written against the background of Genesis 1 and 2. Jesus refers to it, and St. Paul builds doctrine on it. The Bible tells of the supernatural, of which creation is an important part. God is not relatively powerful; He is all-powerful.

Genesis records the beginning of our universe. All subsequent Biblical revelation presupposes a knowledge of the origin of the universe, of life, and man. Often throughout the Old Testament, God is called the Creator of the heavens and the earth, and as such He is worshiped. The Gospel of John begins with the reaffirmation of the creative work of God. Romans opens by showing men that their ignorance of God is inexcusable, because the created universe which surrounds them should suffice as the revelation to them of the invisible things of the Godhead. Paul's epistles exalt Christ as the One by whom the world was framed. Hebrews likewise gives creation a strategic emphasis. Paul points to a faithful Creator as One to whom we can trustfully commit our souls. Destroy the reliability of the Genesis account of creation, and the great structure of the New Testament truth is without foundation and the mission of God is perverted.

The ultimate mystery of the origin of the world confronts

all theories alike. To maintain that the world was created in another way than God's Word declares is placing more faith in another source than God's Word. No science with its backward look ever can take away the ultimate mystery of life. We cannot cut off mystery—the need to trust.

Even though Genesis does not promise to include all sorts of answers to scientifically conceived questions about creation, it does intend to tell the truth. It does not lie. It is accepted as truth by faith. A person who says that the how of creation has nothing to do with the why of creation deceives himself and distorts God's revelation. The Biblical account centers on both the why and how of God's creative power.

To the evolutionist, Adam and Eve cannot be individuals; they must represent an evolutionary group. Yet it is very clear that Moses in Genesis is talking about one man and one woman. St. Paul understands Moses this way: in Romans 5 he repeatedly compares the one Adam with the one Christ (vv. 12, 14, 15, 18, 19). Removal of Adam (made out of dust) from the realm of actual history destroys the validity and trustworthiness of the entire Bible. It indeed is a pivotal doctrine.

"Man became a living soul" (Gen. 2:7) does not allow a prehuman form of life for Adam's body. Adam was not any kind of living creature until he became one by the creative breath of God; God did not breathe His spiritual image into an apelike animal. The God who tells us why He made male and female also tells us how He made them; He tells how He made them perfect, how they perverted this nature, and how He reclaimed them! "And God formed . . ." is not merely figurative and devoid of meaning. Gen. 2:22 tells how God "built" Eve from a portion of Adam's side (1 Cor. 11:8). Once we learn that Eve was created supernaturally (1 Tim. 2:13), the whole purpose of trying to interpret Adam's creation in theistic evolutionary terms collapses. When the Pharisees faced

Jesus with the divorce question (Matt. 19:3), He answered them with Genesis 2:24 and Genesis 1:27.

Creation means that some things had an appearance of age; if you could have done research on the eighth day of the world's existence, you would have found Adam not two days old, but mature in body and mind!

"All flesh is not the same flesh; but there is one flesh of men and another of beasts" (1 Cor. 15:39). Theistic evolution would not agree, for it says that all are derived from the same ancestors, but this clashes with Paul's doctrine of man's physical uniqueness. Presented is a literal miracle of God, not a fictionalized drama or Semitic epic.

God's Word stands above man, nature, and science. "Let there be, and there was!" (Genesis 1).

4. *Some Concerns*

Our youth should study the ever-changing evolutionary theories, and learn that *theories* do not destroy the timeless Biblical truths upon which their faith is built. Evolution can be viewed as a working hypothesis (but not a rejection a priori of Genesis!) but never a satisfactory one by a Christian, who knows the truth of his Creator by faith. Science is forced to devise theories, though sometimes weak and unproved, but it is impossible to synthesize them with Biblical truths. Around us are some major church bodies who generally have adapted Biblical interpretation to evolutionary theories.

Emotionalism pleads that evolutionism be permitted because some Christians who accept it have not lost their faith in Christ—or God has not thundered down His wrath on them. When we have failed to proclaim the Word clearly enough to give our youth a proper understanding, we are inflicting on them a cruel hoax as we advise them to compromise the Biblical truth to match certain theories in order to "appear reasonable." Science is unable to challenge the doctrine of Creation any more than the doctrine of the Incarnation, the Trinity, or Regeneration.

The Biblical and scientific realms have two different definitions of truth. The Bible is independent of science. Because in past history some churchmen made the mistake of making unwarranted observations, as in the day of Galileo, we should not repeat their mistakes. Rather, we rejoice over every additional discovery by science and are saddened only when it is misinterpreted and abused to the hurt of mankind, if God is not given proper recognition.

The supernaturalistic creation view does not hamper the search for learning but encourages it, as Luther did in his day. Within science the controversy regarding evolutionism is continuing, but let it remain outside of the church. Give the natural man no pulpit in Christ's church.

There is nothing to fear from true science. However, we should be wary of pseudoscience, which transgresses the limits set by sound scientific procedures and the realm of scientific method, which must deal only with observable phonomena and with the measurement and experimental testing of them. Science and the Bible are separate in subject and method. Neither depends on the other.

Reason is man's God-given ability for receiving, organizing, and evaluating knowledge and experience. By the Word, however, reason is taken captive in Christ. His Word is the sole criterion for evaluating what we find in the world.

Scientific findings have been a great blessing to man. They are even a greater blessing to the church since they offer Christ's workers transportation, communication, healing of body, and other matters in service to God. Let science serve the Christians in their mission, rather than question the Word that sends men on that mission. Many competent scientists are "creationists" (accept the Genesis account by faith); some have formed a Creation Science Research Society.[17]

Francis Schaeffer, the most prolific Christian writer of our day, affirms that historic Christianity has something important to say to the modern world. Schaeffer contends that only historic Christianity, rightly understood and fearlessly applied, can solve the dilemmas of modern man in an age of existentialism and new theologies.

Francis and Edith Schaeffer, together with their family, maintain L'Abri in Huemos nur Ollon, Switzerland, a vital community and warm fellowship, where philosophic answers are given to people's problems on the basis of the Christian faith. With other workers in Milan, London, Amsterdam, France, and America, the L'Abri family desires "to show forth, by demonstration in our life and work, the existence of God." They insist that to establish the reality of God's existence is not a matter of reasonable proof on the intellectual level alone, but a matter also of showing that the God "who is there" is active in answer to specific prayer on the part of His own people.

Many remarkable circumstances have brought young people to visit or study in the tiny Swiss village, people having many backgrounds of nationality and color and belief: atheists, agnostics, existentialists, Hindus, Jews, Roman Catholics, liberal Protestants, Buddhists, and many more who have accepted the relativistic thinking of the 20th century.

Schaeffer demonstrates how the new humanism and new theology fit into the complex history of modern thought and culture, nontheological as well as theological. He gives a panoramic sweep of the last 200 years of Western and Eastern thinking, and helps many who have drifted off into the byways of non-Christian sectarian thought and movements.

Many evangelicals believe that Schaeffer is a man to whom God has given a special gift of understanding the mentality of the 20th century and of identifying himself with people affected by it. He holds a position where he can brilliantly expose the 20th-century mentality and yet also sympathetically find ways of giving the only answers which could possibly satisfy people's deepest longings for order and reality in their lives.

Such books as *True Spirituality, Escape from Reason,* and *The God Who Is There* are intended as an exposé of the bankruptcy of both secular and modern theological thought and hold out a well-founded hope that man will again find his real personality and purpose if he will only turn to the life-giving Word which God has communicated in the Scriptures. His writings and lectures help people understand their own relationships with God better and also equip them to live out and communicate the Christian faith more realistically and effectively.

In answer to our question concerning the unique and radical mission of L'Abri, Schaeffer wrote: "When L'Abri began, Edith and I and our family felt that we should offer ourselves to the Lord to ask Him to use us as a demonstration that He exists in our generation. We have tried to hold to this constantly in the intervening 20 years.

"1. As a part of this call we felt that we should never ask for funds but only pray for them.

"2. We felt we should not have a developed plan for the work but simply follow along as the Lord opens doors for us. Thus we had no special plans for the work such as L'Abri has become, but this is just simply what has developed from the basis of those the Lord has sent to us and their friends that they in their turn sent to us.

"3. We committed ourselves to praying that the Lord would bring whom He would and keep others away.

"4. Concerning the staff, we thought it was our calling not to go out and look for staff members but to simply pray for them.

"It should be noted that we do not think this way of operation is higher than any other way of operation the Lord leads His people into, but it is simply the way we felt the Lord would have us to work as a demonstration of His own existence.

"What L'Abri has become known as is a place where the intellectual, cultural, and practical problems of the 20th century are brought in contact with the historic Christian answers.

"I would visualize Christianity as being unique in the concept of an infinite personal God who has given revelation to man in verbalized, propositional form. God is personal on the high level of Trinity, and He has not remained silent but rather has spoken to us in the Bible and given us propositional truth not only in the area of what men usually consider religious but also where the Bible speaks of history and the cosmos. The Eastern gods may be by definition considered infinite but they are not personal. The Western gods tend to be thought of as personal but not infinite. Mohammedanism has no unity or diversity in God because they have no Trinity, and Mohammedanism has no answers as to how God can be holy yet accept sinful man, because there is no Savior.

"To me the church should be two things, that is, have two orthodoxies. First of all there should be an orthodoxy of doctrine, which above all else means a faithfulness to the Scriptures. Secondly, there should be an orthodoxy of community in that the church should provide a community in the whole of life, including the caring of each other in material needs."

Notes to Chapter 12

[1] Francis A. Schaeffer, *Escape from Reason* (Downers Grove, Ill.: Inter-Varsity, 1968), p. 55.

[2] C. S. Lewis, *Mere Christianity* (New York: Macmillan, 1943).

[3] 1 Cor. 1:17; 3:3, 21.

[4] R. A. Torrey, *The Importance and Value of Proper Bible Study* (Chicago: Moody Press, 1921), p. 67.

[5] Ex. 20:1-6; Is. 10:10-11; Acts 19:18-19.

[6] Rom. 1:19-21; 3:23; Eph. 2:1-3.

[7] John 5:24; Rom. 1:16; 3:22; 10:5, 13; Eph. 2:12; Phil. 3:9; 2 Thess. 1:8-10.

[8] Tappert Edition, 419:66.

[9] Ibid., 367:19.

[10] Ibid., 19:1; 20:27-28; 21:40.

[11] Francis A. Schaeffer, *The God Who Is There* (Downers Grove, Ill.: Inter-Varsity, 1968).

[12] Norman L. Geisler, *Christ: The Theme of the Bible* (Chicago: Moody Press, Moody Bible Institute of Chicago, 1968; used by permission), p. 11.

[13] Ibid., pp. 26, 23, 24.

[14] Ewald Plass, *What Luther Says* (St. Louis: Concordia, 1959), p. 1480, No. 4783.

[15] C. S. Lewis, *Miracles* (New York: Macmillan, 1947), pp. 170 ff.

[16] Ps. 102:25-26; Rom. 8:19-22; 1 Peter 1:24; 2 Peter 3:12-13.

[17] Information, materials, and membership available: Creation Science Research Center, 4250 Pacific Highway, Suite 117, San Diego, CA 92110. Among the representative books available are: Henry M. Morris, *The Remarkable Birth of Planet Earth* (Minneapolis: Bethany Fellowship, 1974). Another creationist group which offers a large number of excellent materials is the Bible—Science Association, Inc., Box 1016, Caldwell, Idaho 83605.

Chapter 13

A Confessional and Confessing Church

As a church establishes a common agreement, goals, and tasks for its mission in a confession, constitution, and by-laws, it makes a confession to the world as to how it stands towards God's Word and the saving Gospel of Jesus Christ and how it proposes to perform its radical mission in the world.

What is a confessing church? Such a church is one that lives what it believes, practices what it preaches, teaches what it professes, and actually uses the Word of God in its daily life as both a healing and motivating power. The confessing church not only has a confessional basis in its written documents but actually confesses its beliefs openly and vigorously.

Courage in confessing is essential when the presence of doctrinal error or apparent indifference to pure doctrine threatens the church's continuing commitment to the truth of God's Word and its very mission. Both of these problems are evident in many churches today. Most churches can no longer assume either the doctrinal unity of their membership or its total commitment to the historic Biblical faith. The point in question is the authority and nature of the Holy Scriptures, their inspiration and infallibility.

Christian faith is dependent on sound doctrine. Our faith in Jesus Christ and His Gospel is simultaneously faith that Jesus Christ did in fact live, die, and rise again for our justification and eternal life. Take away this doctrinal content of faith, and the church as a divine institution is destroyed. Jude's admonition is the abiding watchword of the confessing church: "Contend for the faith which was once for all delivered to the saints" (v. 3 RSV).

Theologians should lead churches in a creative exposition of the Word (the Holy Scriptures in their entirety) for the mission programs and opportunities and theological concerns of our day. A united effort based on a sound confessionalism is required, which at the same time is a dynamic confessionalism in the form of Gospel proclamation to the non-Christian masses. We can ill afford theological arguments that neither edify nor build the Kingdom.

It may well be that "speaking the truth in love" amidst doctrinal disagreements will be misunderstood or even challenged. Some may regard positive activity on behalf of the truth and unity of the church as negativism, or "protest action," or even as reactionary divisiveness. Attempts to overcome and heal doctrinal error are not to cause disunity or to be divisive, anymore than the proper diagnosis of a disease is to be confused with its cause.

The church is to exercise its legitimate right of united defense against unscriptural doctrine and schism. It dare not be distracted by those who belittle the church's responsibility to discipline those who betray the fellowship as expressed in the public doctrine of the church. This doctrine should be reflected faithfully with creative conviction by all church institutions, publications, agencies, departments, as well as auxiliaries and affiliates.

The confessing church presents clearly the facts of God's Word and the testimony of its confessions in all situations, evangelically, winsomely, and with love. It should speak clearly and unequivocally, not using words or phrases with dual meanings or coming to inconclusive decisions.

It has become popular in some church circles to claim openmindedness in presenting issues by portraying the "pros" and "cons" and then ending with a synthesis of ideas, leaving the reader or listener to make a choice. This will not be true of the confessional or confessing church.

Fidelity is required in the church's classrooms: Opposing views of different scholars that allow the student to make up his mind as to what he will accept cannot be tolerated.

Fidelity is required in all dialogs, discussions, and in disciplinary cases: It is not a question or argument between two opposing points of view. Only and solely, the church's Confession must be brought to bear on every situation, difficult or easy—that is the question!

Faithful Seminaries

Faithful Christians will expect vital congregations shepherded by faithful pastors who are trained by evangelical seminaries. Like seminary, like pastor.

Paul wrote to his faithful disciple, young Timothy: "The things that thou hast heard of me among many witnesses, the same commit thou to faithful men, who shall be able to teach others also" (2 Tim. 2:2). If the orthodox evangelical faith is to be communicated from the church of one generation to another, the ministers must be educated to know what the Bible is, what the human mind is, and how to bring one to influence the other. When a seminary demonstrates great fidelity to Biblical truth, it will be a center for the renewal of the church.

Academic freedom does not give a seminary the right to change the theological position of the supporting church body. A church seminary may not be used as a tool for the advancement of the new theology or for propagating modifications in doctrine and practice. On the contrary, it should be used as God's instrument and the church's proper vehicle to serve the church faithfully for defining, teaching, and declaring the truths of the Scriptures. Professors who accept the church's call to equip and send out candidates for the office of the public ministry are held by honesty, integrity, and simple duty to abide by the public doctrine of their church in their teaching. This does not preclude inquiry and research in any area. Theological education is to be subject to the authority of the Word of God.

Publications

Because of its Christian commitment, the Christian press will reflect the best journalistic standards and the standards of God's holy Word. "If any man speak, let him speak as the oracles of God" (1 Peter 4:11) applies to everyone who expresses an opinion regarding a subject on which "the oracles of God" (Rom. 3:2) have spoken. This applies with special force to the publications of a church body when those publications are designed to edify and build up the faith of the people.

The Lord Jesus said: "Judge righteous judgment!" (John 7:24). When a church publication pronounces judgment regarding a spiritual matter, its judgment is required to be in total agreement with the Scriptures, the basis of the church's fellowship.

A church publication which observes this principle will enable the reader to receive not mere human opinions only but reliable messages from the Lord Jesus through the Scriptures. Only as a publication interprets news and events via editorial policies in tune with the Scriptures has it served the church and its purpose. Thus it will not be a promotional tool for influencing the readers to adopt a new or permissive attitude on any Scriptural matter beyond the common agreement accepted by the church itself.

Confess Boldly and Gladly

The confession of a church is a declaration of commitment to itself and to its members. To be a confessional church means that its members believe certain doctrines to be an essential part of the Christian faith and promise to adhere to these doctrines and to preach and to teach them. This does not mean that a particular church body does not recognize other evangelical faiths as a part of the Christian family.

Being confessional and confessing is not in opposition to progress or aggressive mission. Rather, it is in opposition to making changes in basics of Christian faith and practice.

The confessional church needs a process whereby legitimate dissent can be heard and studied. It is imperative that members who disagree with the historic position of a church use that process, not ignore it and organize cliques and groups to hold opposing positions. The church has a right to hold a collective opinion and to set up a community of the likeminded. Since no man joins it on his own terms, he may not change it on his own terms. However, great care should be taken that the voice of the church is not simply the echo of our own voices but of the truth of God.

A Confessing Church is one that believes that what God says is more important than what man thinks, one that cherishes truth more than inquiry, one that seeks not popular acclaim to bask in it, one that is concerned about preserving the Gospel heritage and about sharing it with the entire world.

The confessing church will be an inclusive church — as inclusive as "Come unto Me, all ye that labor." The confessing church will also be exclusive — excluding those whom Christ excludes because of unbelief, persistent error, and resistance to God's Word. However, the confessing church today strives with redoubled vigor to reach all these in compassion, as does Christ.

Great today is the need for trumpeting confessions of the Gospel, relevant to the issues of the contemporary theological apostasy but subordinate to and subject to the authentic Scriptures. They will be honest expositions of the Christian faith and articulate a healing mission to the world.

Chapter 14

The Harvest is Now

WHERE'S THE HARVEST?

We shall have a clear vision of the world if the lense we use is the Word of God. Through this lense we shall "lift up our eyes to look on the fields . . . white to harvest" (John 4:35). Our life mission is founded on the Word and focused on the world.

Christ knew His world, engaged it, was killed by it, yet overcame it and saved it. Jesus said: "Truly, truly, I say to you, unless a grain of wheat falls into the earth and dies, it remains alone; but if it dies, it bears much fruit. He who loves his life loses it, and he who hates his life in this world will keep it for eternal life" (John 12:24-25 RSV). Only as we by faith plant our lives, our minds, our personalities, our abilities, our time, our voices, our all into the ground of life like a grain of wheat will we produce hundredfold. If we do not plant ourselves through our witness and service of Christ under the Word, we shall die without reproducing ourselves in any form or fashion —a worthless life.

Genesis stresses the fact of capacity for reproduction as the sign or proof of the continuation and development of life. Life finds its purpose and fulfillment in reproduction, for when God created the first plants and animals, each had in it "seed according to its kind." The Bible uses such words as "field . . . seed . . . sower . . . reaper . . . seedtime . . . harvest," and applies them spiritually to Christian witness and spiritual reproduction. The parable of nature becomes the life story of grace: "The field is the world; the good seed are the children of the Kingdom" (Matt. 13:38).

Every believer is a seed of God for the world field and for the final harvest. As the body is reproduced from another body, so spiritual life is reproduced through the instrument of another spiritual life using the Word of God supplied by the Holy Spirit. The good seed is the Word of God by the Holy Spirit. The good seed is the Word of God, which finds reception in the heart and is developed fully. After germination, then growth, then fruit: "First the blade, then the ear, then the full-grown corn in the ear."

There is to be a death of the seed if it is to attain its divine purpose and destiny. What is the death? Only death to the old self, the things of the world, wasted hours, bad habits, poor relationships, idle rituals, laziness, self-interest, self-indulgence, self-advantage—all are laid on the altar of service to Christ. This death is the voluntary sacrifice of self-interest generated by the power of the Holy Spirit.

The result is a great spiritual harvest. This, too, is radical and supernatural. The man of the world reproduces nothing, even though in his humanitarian acts he may help some people materially for a time. At the end of the world all of this will be burned, gone. Only faith and the soul will count.

Biologically, the harvest has multiplied unbelievably from 1930 to 1975, from 2 billion to 4 billion people. Spiritually, there has been no multiplication, only a little addition. In 1930 less than a billion confessed Christ. In 1975 hardly more than a billion confessed Christ. Spiritually, by the Spirit of God, we need to learn geometric progression. That's the law of the harvest. Every harvest provides "seed for the sower as well as bread for the eater," and so there is joy and strength as new converts are added, multiplying through successive crops. He who shares God's Word with the non-Christian sets in motion a Christian witness that multiplies infinitely and eternally.

In view of this great spiritual harvest to be reaped, we need to set an infinite value on the soul of every person in the world, to encourage a fresh vision of the evangelistic nature of the mission and of the necessity of every Christian everywhere to share the Gospel, to have an awareness of mission dangers and mission potentials, and to use aggressive mission methods in discipling the nations for which we have accepted responsibility.

The missionary era is not at an end, but will be enlarged as we take more seriously the Great Commission of Jesus. We will do well to administer our world missions in the spirit of Paul, who for three years with many tears did not cease night or day to admonish, and to commend the church and members to God and to the Word of His grace, which is able to build up and give eternal inheritance to those who believe (Acts 20:31-32).

It is time to "declare war on spiritual poverty" the world around. The world in which we live needs nothing more than Gospel messengers called by God, who tell about the way of salvation. It is intolerable that any human being alive should live without ever having the chance to hear and receive it. How can we discharge our debt to all men except to "declare war on spiritual poverty," a poverty which forces people to live with no personal God on whom to call, no divine purpose, no meaning to their days and years — nothing except the inexorable law of cause and effect, no Savior from sin.

In this kind of world, "The best we can give is the Gospel in our day," declares Oswald J. Smith. We have great organizational power (sometimes used in side affairs), financial power (sometimes not used fully and effectively), and workers (many of whom are not in the field). Human love alone will not do the job, but only God's love and the power of His Word.

St. Paul reminds us of the sacred responsibility laid upon us and how we are entrusted with the Gospel. Our Savior speaks of working "while it is day" before "night comes when no man can work," when opportunities are gone (John 9:4). We can stimulate a greater faithfulness in discerning where the ripened harvest fields are and where more missionaries are to be sent forth, converts are to be won, and churches are to be established. The Book of Acts shows the believers always sending someone to some faraway place. An assignment of this magnitude requires soul-searching and analysis.

The sacred responsibility laid upon us means that we cannot be satisfied by settling for a token presence in each country rather than a serious attempt to fulfill the full command of Christ. While we rejoice over a few sheaves of gathered grain, we will not ignore the massive harvest still standing in the fields. We thrill over the accounts of missionary sacrifices, but we must insist on a parade of witnesses in regions beyond, just as the Holy Spirit forced Peter beyond the ethnic limitations of Judaism. As the Holy Spirit instructed the church at Antioch to send forth the best leaders they had (Paul and Barnabas) so that the regions of Asia and Europe might learn the Gospel, so the only hope for the total evangelization of the world is to teach the Christian believers of each nation to evangelize and missionize.

We affirm that God is working in the world by His Word. He is not limited. His Word is reliable and amazingly powerful. He uses ordinary people to do extraordinary work. His compassion for the lost compels us to press forward. This supernatural mission is God's, and He has enlisted all believers.

What is your need to be a dynamic witness for Christ? to be compelled supernaturally in your mission, to be a seed that will reproduce a hundredfold? "My God shall supply all your need according to His riches in glory by Christ Jesus!" (Phil. 4:19).

What are we to do to make the most of our hours and days in service to our Savior? Identify the whole human race and every unevangelized area of the world, including our own neighborhood, as a mission field for the saving Gospel of Jesus Christ. Broaden our horizons so that we do not think only locally but globally. Present a sure Word from God and share our Christian faith, not debate it.

Formulas and strategies are not enough. We need to draw closer to the Flame of God, believing and obeying His Word. By the power of the Holy Spirit we need to move out from our worship services and the comfort of our local fellowship to our larger parish—the entire world of lost men. Through practical witness and activities we must find ways to put wheels and wings on our song, "Let the earth hear His voice!"

Someone at the International Congress on World Evangelization in Lausanne said that our God has spoken, and He says, "Move!" Genesis 12:1 tells us that God said to Abraham, "Get out!" Urgent is our task to move out from the comfort of our homes and routines into the great harvest field of the world.

The harvest is NOW!